FASHION SCHOOL

I0109976

IN A BOOK

DESIGN

ZOË HONG

THE **PRACTICAL**
WORKBOOK
FOR COLLECTION
DEVELOPMENT

JOURNAL

Fashion School in a Book Design Journal

The Practical Workbook for Collection Development

Zoë Hong
Zoehong.com

Project editor: Maggie Yates
Project manager: Lisa Brazieal
Marketing coordinator: Koryn Olage
Copyeditor: Maggie Yates
Layout: Kim Scott, Bumpy Design
Cover and interior design: Frances Baca

ISBN: 979-8-88814-237-0
1st Edition (1st printing, January 2025)
© 2025 Zoë Hong
All images © Zoë Hong

Rocky Nook Inc.
1010 B Street, Suite 350
San Rafael, CA 94901
USA

www.rockynook.com

Distributed in the UK and Europe by Publishers Group UK
Distributed in the U.S. and all other territories by Publishers Group West

Library of Congress Control Number: 2024937112

Printed in China

TABLE OF CONTENTS

Introduction, 1

1   Fashion Design Process Overview, 5

2   Brand Direction, 9

3   Collection Direction, 23

4   Color, 57

5   Print Development and Surface Design, 73

6   Fabric, 97

7   Shapes and Silhouettes, 111

8   3-D Development, 147

9   Merchandising and Editing, 171

10   Beyond Design Process for Brands, 191

11   Portfolios, 195

INTRODUCTION

Hey hey, party people!

This Design Journal is for the ones who are ready to get to work.

You've read some books, maybe you've read my book. You've watched my YouTube videos. You've amassed some knowledge and chicken-scratched on a million little pieces of paper. And now you're ready to start a proper design project.

I put together this workbook to help you get organized and stay organized. I put this workbook in order of the fashion design process. I stuffed it full of design prompts and exercises and blank templates for you to sketch designs, track your fabrics and trims, and practice renderings.

Forget everything you've seen on social media: pristine, gorgeous, meticulous pages with no mistakes. Real life, and real fashion design, is messier than someone's highlight reel on social media. Perfectionism is stupid and is the opposite of progress. And when you get tired or discouraged, you don't have to chase down all your random bits and bobs; they'll all be here, ready for you to pick up where you left off.

This Design Journal is for the ones who are ready to walk the walk. Now get to work.

Love,
Zoë

Ruin the first page.
Perfectionism prevents progress.
#perfectionismisstupid

·

1
FASHION DESIGN PROCESS OVERVIEW

BRAND

INSPIRATION

COLOR

PRINTS

FABRIC & TEXTURES

SHAPES & SILHOUETTES

DESIGN DETAILS

EDIT

inspiration, colors, fabrics, motifs
detailed into design direction
by creative director
&
sample yardage of fabrics/trims ordered

print designers apply
direction to prints

designers apply direction to
individual garments
+ draw flats

meetings to approve +
discard designs

approved designs made into tech packs
approved prints made into
sample yardgage

more designs
until you have enough
for a collection
(+ a few spares)

sampling process
including
patterns
sewn samples
fittings etc.

approved designs
made into tech packs,
etc.

sampling process
etc.

wholesale:
photograph samples to
produce sales materials
for trade shows, runway shows,
sales meetings, social media

collect orders,
run production
based on orders

direct to consumer:
photograph samples to
update stores, website,
social media

run production based on
prior sales numbers

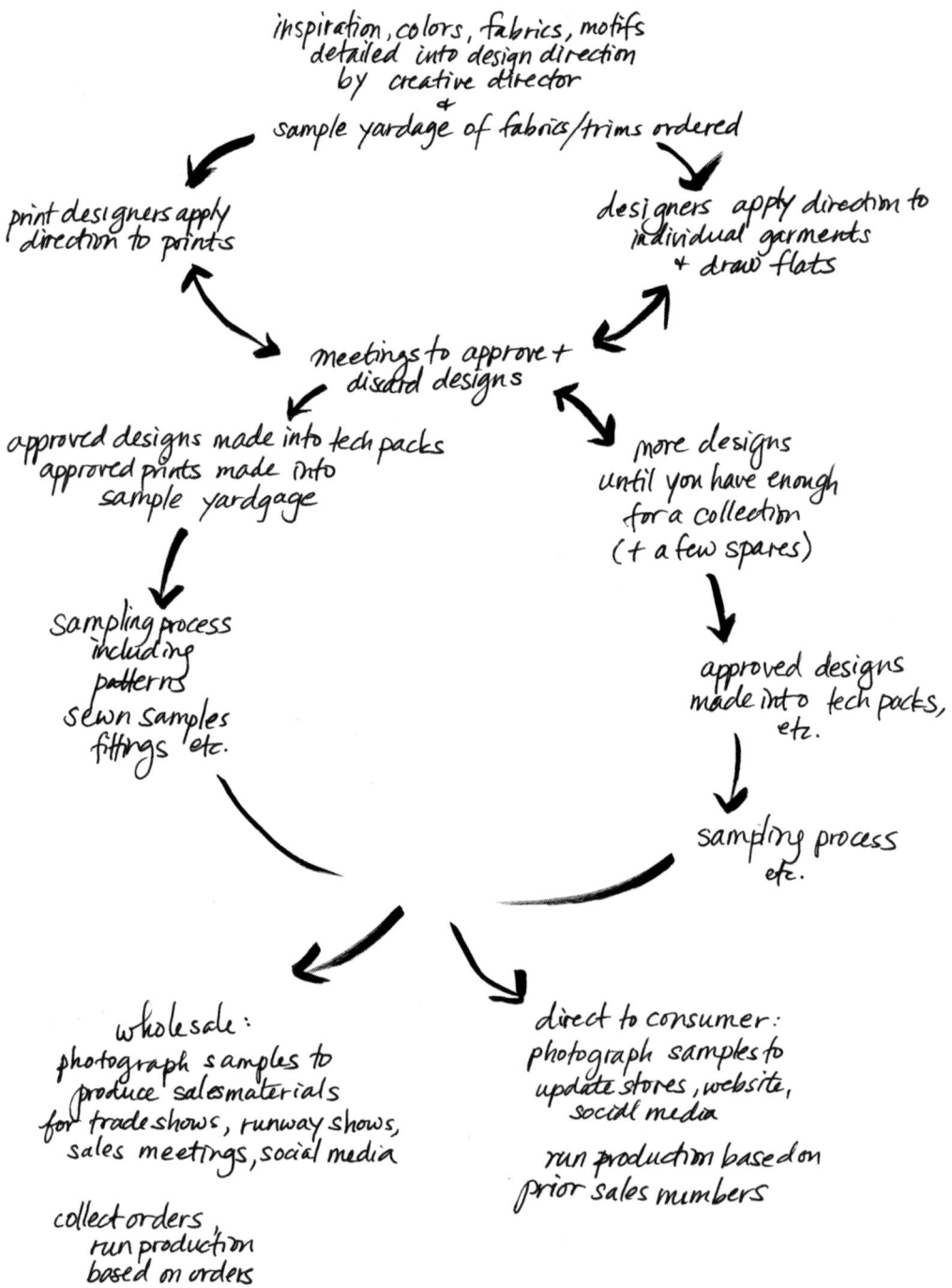

Design process for brands

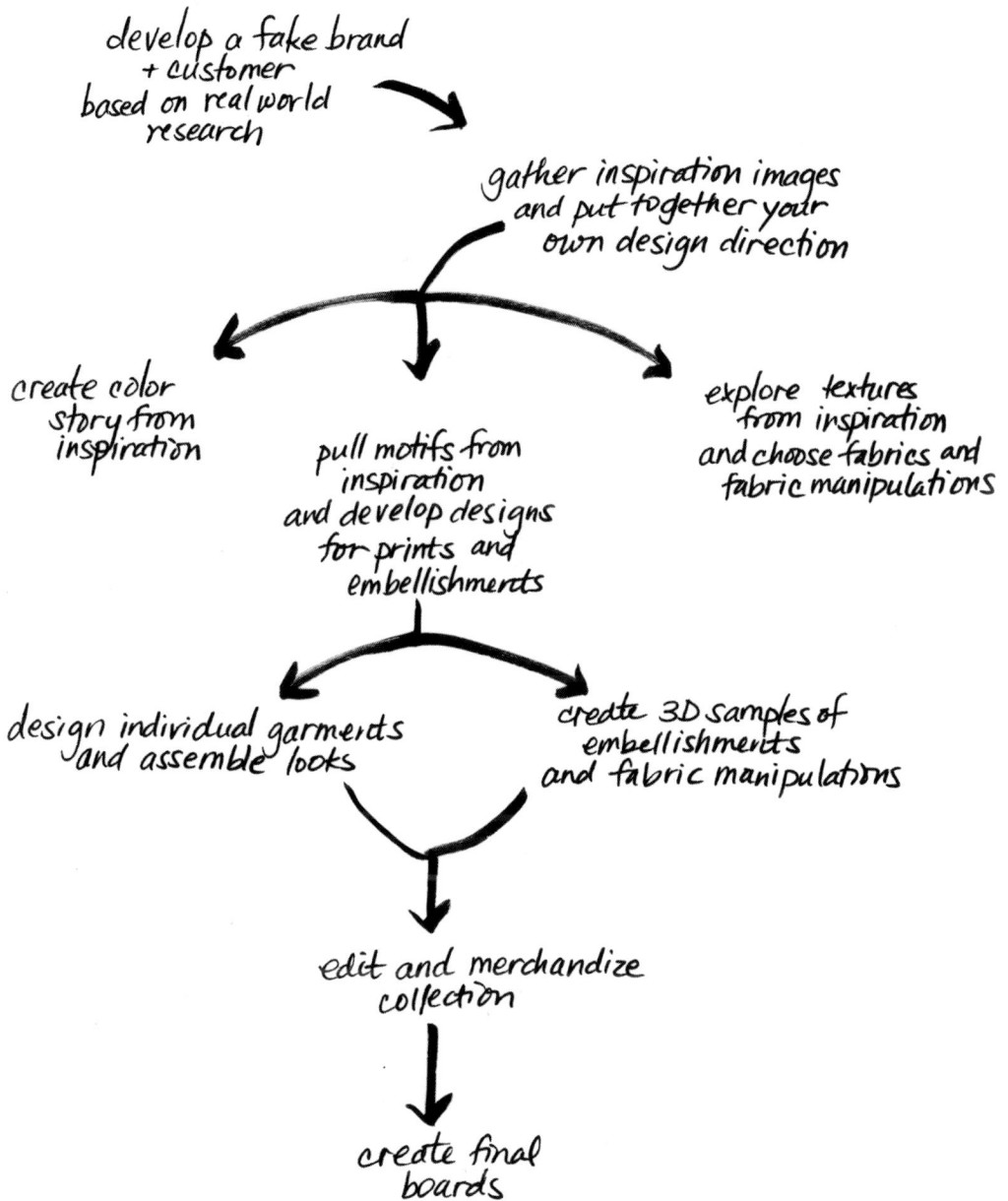

develop a fake brand
+ customer
based on real world
research

gather inspiration images
and put together your
own design direction

create color
story from
inspiration

pull motifs from
inspiration
and develop designs
for prints and
embellishments

explore textures
from inspiration
and choose fabrics and
fabric manipulations

design individual garments
and assemble looks

create 3D samples of
embellishments
and fabric manipulations

edit and merchandize
collection

create final
boards

Design process for portfolio projects

2

BRAND DIRECTION

START THINKING ABOUT WHAT KIND OF BRAND YOU WANT TO BUILD:

What kind of clothes do you want to make?

_____

_____

_____

What garment category do you want to start with? Sweaters? Cocktail dresses? Jeans?

_____

What price point/market category is your brand?

_____

_____

What do you think will set your brand apart from other brands? What value do you want to bring to the world?

_____

_____

_____

Are there any elements you think would make for a house code? A color you love?

_____

_____

Any symbols that are meaningful to you? Any good luck symbols, animals, or flowers?

_____

_____

Have you thought about how to incorporate sustainability in your brand? Through materials? Through processes? Through business practices?

_____

_____

_____

_____

_____

Do you want to build a wholesale business or a direct-to-consumer business? Think about the pros and cons that affect you directly.

_____

_____

What are some things you learned in your industry research that directly affects your brand?

_____

_____

_____

_____

_____

BRAND VALUES

	1	2	3	4
_____	1	2	3	4
_____	1	2	3	4
_____	1	2	3	4
_____	1	2	3	4
_____	1	2	3	4
_____	1	2	3	4
_____	1	2	3	4
_____	1	2	3	4
_____	1	2	3	4
_____	1	2	3	4
_____	1	2	3	4
_____	1	2	3	4

1 = not essential but would be nice to include

2 = important, moderate priority

3 = high priority

4 = absolutely essential to my brand

CUSTOMER PROFILE:

Who is your muse and why/how do they inspire you?

_____

_____

What is the age and gender(s) of your customer?

_____

What is your average customer income? How do they spend their money?

_____

_____

_____

What is your product price point?

_____

What is your customer's body type and size range?

_____

_____

What is your customer's lifestyle? Where do they live? What are their jobs and everyday activities? What are they doing while wearing your clothes or accessories?

_____

_____

_____

_____

Does your product help your customer engage in specific activities like hiking boots or nursing bras? Explain specific product performance and materials needs.

_____

_____

What is your customer's attitude toward your product category? If your product is a backpack, what is your customer's attitude toward backpacks? When and how often does your customer use your type of backpack? What do they need from a backpack?

_____

_____

_____

_____

How does your customer make their shopping decisions? Is price the most important? Shopping convenience? Exclusive products? Does your customer shop for trends or classic investment pieces? Do they trust peer reviews, or do they trust big fashion journalism outlets like magazines?

_____

_____

_____

_____

_____

Where does your customer shop? What kinds of stores and what websites?

_____

_____

_____

Who or what is your competition at the same price point? What would make your product better than theirs?

_____

_____

_____

_____

What else is your customer wearing? Let's say you're making party shoes. If your customer's going out on a date and wearing your shoes, what brands and kinds of clothes are they wearing? What jewelry are they wearing? Imagine your muse in the whole look.

_____

_____

_____

What media does your customer consume? What TV and radio stations, which social media platforms, what podcasts, etc., do they use that can influence their lifestyles and shopping decisions?

_____

_____

_____

Illustrate your muse and customer. What does their body look like? Put that body in a pose that shows off your muse's attitude.

Alternatively, make a collage of photos of people you would love to dress with your brand, people you think illustrate your customer well. These people do not need to be famous. They can be random style shots from Pinterest or photos of your mom or a stylish friend.

An "elevator pitch" is a short speech encapsulating why your business idea is the best and worth people's attention and time. An elevator pitch should be less than 30 seconds. Write it here.

_____

_____

_____

_____

_____

_____

_____

_____

_____

_____

_____

_____

_____

_____

_____

_____

_____

_____

_____

_____

_____

_____

PRODUCT ANALYSIS:

Choose an item of the same type as your brand/project and analyze the construction by answering the questions below. Analyze at least one product in your price point, one more expensive, and one less expensive. Take photos of the analysis process for your own reference.

Describe the product.

_____

_____

What is the price?

_____

Fabric? Fiber content?

_____

_____

Knit, woven, hide, nonwoven?

_____

_____

Is the fabric high quality? Is it itchy or soft? Is it rough in a cool way or a bad way?

_____

_____

Is there a print? Is it well done? With solid dyes/pigments soaked into the fabric, no weird gaps, and printed straight on the fabric?

_____

_____

_____

Check the seams. Are they well sewn? Look for smooth, neat seams, not loose, gaping stitches; no weird bunching or puckering. The seams should be straight or clean curves, not wonky, ripply, or wavy. Do the seams itch when the garment is worn or when you run your hand over them?

_____

_____

_____

Are there any trims? Are zippers and buttons high quality and sewn on securely? Do zippers pull smoothly? Do the buttonhole stitches look neat and tight? Are hooks and eyes sewn on securely? Are snaps punched in without puckering the fabric?

_____

_____

_____

_____

Are there any embellishments? Run your hand over the beading. Does it feel like beads are about to fall loose? Are the embroidery stitches tight and smooth? With high-quality embroidery, you should not be able to see the fabric in between the threads. Are patches sewn on securely?

_____

_____

_____

Are there pockets? Are they real or fake pockets? Are the pockets a decent size with strong construction?

_____

_____

_____

Look inside. Is it lined? Is the lining fabric good quality? What's the lining's fiber content?

_____

_____

If not lined, how are the seams finished? Overlock? Hong Kong finish? Is the stitching neat and professional?

_____

_____

_____

Try it on and analyze the fit. Or have a friend try it on. Does it pinch or rub anywhere? Does the fabric pull weirdly? Walk around and sit in it. Is it comfortable? Does the garment move with you?

_____

_____

_____

_____

_____

Does the hangtag include repair extras like extra buttons or beads?

_____

_____

Is this product worth the price? Why or why not?

_____

_____

_____

_____

3

COLLECTION DIRECTION

The following pages detail some possible design briefs you can use to start developing your collection direction. Start taking some exploratory notes in the accompanying blank pages. If none of these appeal to you, I have included a list of activities and places to visit to help inspire you.

DESIGN BRIEF 1: TWO BECOME ONE

Pick two vastly different time periods. Choose some elements from each and merge them into a cohesive, modern collection that doesn't look like costume design.

Each time period should be as short as possible. Fashion moves very fast today, but there were times in history when people wore the same things for hundreds of years. Clothing in Western Europe didn't change all that much throughout the 14th century, so you can use that as one time period; but, if you pick the 20th century, you have to pick a specific decade. Fashion in the '40s looked very different from fashion in the '20s. I wager the concept of microtrends are wholly a post-internet phenomenon.

You can and should select different countries as well. It is best if you use just a few elements from each time period and country, instead of trying to cram too many styles into one collection. We are being inspired, not copying or translating.

Examples: Merge elements from 1950s China and 1890s USA. Early 1400s France and modern-day Tokyo. The Inca Empire and 1970s Iran. 1920s Golden Age Hollywood and Mars 200 years in the future. Choose even smaller subcultures than what I've listed, such as the Teddy Boys, a mainly British subculture of 1950s and 1960s youth.

Pick up a costume history book at your local library and flip through until you spy something cool.

DESIGN BRIEF 2: MASTER OF SOMEONE ELSE'S DOMAIN

Select a brand and pretend you have been hired to be their new creative director. Design a collection for this brand. How can you pay homage to the history of the brand while looking forward and creating something new? Start by studying the brand's history.

Example: Gucci has a history of craftsmanship, especially beautiful leather work. OG Gucci man, Guccio Gucci, used to work at the Savoy Hotel in London. He returned to Italy to make his own versions of the luxury luggage he saw at the hotel. Some of his earliest works included saddles and other accessories for horsemen. That's what inspired the horse-bit buckles and red and green strapping on his non-equestrian pieces, two things that continue to be Gucci's most famous emblems.

Can you whisper back to that heritage without making your designs look like you're reworking old pieces? Study how other Gucci designers have approached this dilemma, how they have added their own flair and flavor to Gucci. Ford, Giannini, Michele, and De Sarno have all taken that Gucci heritage and run with it, putting their own visual stamps on the house. Take notes on what you can bring to Gucci, how you can marry your aesthetic with Gucci's, and move them into the future.

Pick a house, any house, but maybe not your absolutely favorite house. Some students feel a little too precious about their favorites and have a hard time casting a critical view on the house's history.

DESIGN BRIEF 3: UNICHROMATIC

Fine, "unichromatic" isn't a real word but monochromatic color schemes consist of the main color (red) and its tints (pink!), shades (maroon!), and tones (mauve!). When I say one color, I mean one, singular, all by itself, singing karaoke on a Tuesday night, all alone, color.

Create a collection that is all one color. Use as few variations on the color as possible. If you pick blue, try to stick to one blue, instead of using lots of shades of blue. Create visual interest with textures, shapes, embellishments, fabric manipulations like smocking, pleats, quilting, and tucks. Bonus: don't pick a neutral!

Double points if you choose one fabric. Try one shade of denim, smoky pale pink leather, orange corduroy, sage green linen—anything goes!

I am aware you typically can't just sell one color across your whole store. The point of this exercise is to learn how to create visual interest without relying on color. Ultimately, you will choose some other colors to merchandise out your collection.

DESIGN BRIEF 4: FANGIRL IT OUT

Pick an artist and choose one to four of their works. Pull inspiration from these pieces and create a collection that doesn't look like a series of the artist's reproductions. Do not use too many works; focus and deep dive into a few key pieces. The artist does not have to be famous; the works do not have to be the artist's most well-known pieces.

Do not do anything obvious like screen-printing paintings onto t-shirts or embroidering parts of a painting onto a dress. Do not take things too literally. Go deeper. Research the meanings behind the works.

Take inspiration from Salvador Dali's melting clocks and instead of making beaded clocks, think about elements falling apart, falling down, dissolving. Do not look at Degas's dancers and literally make dance costumes. Be inspired by the color palette, how many colors go into depicting white. Be inspired by the mood of his paintings and sculptures, the gracefulness.

Do not take Keith Haring's people and make it into a print. I mean, first of all, you'll likely be sued. Instead, be inspired by his bright colors, bold lines, political statements, his guerilla style of spreading his work. Take Picasso's *The Bull*. It's a series of 11 lithographs that study the process of abstraction. Do not make a print of bulls or make headdresses with antlers. Consider the meaning of a dress and the many ways you can abstract a dress in varying degrees of intensity.

DESIGN BRIEF 5: WORDPLAY

With your eyes closed, flip through a book. Choose a book with a lot of text on every page. With your eyes still closed, randomly point to a word. Design a collection inspired the definition of that word and what you think about when you read that word. Use a real paper book with pages. If you say you don't have a book, I don't believe you. You're literally reading one right now. (Or support your local library!)

This doesn't really work the same online or on an e-reader. You can try again if you land on more non-descriptive, sentence structure words like "and," "to," or "there." The best words are the ones you didn't know before, so your research is truly fresh.

Or you can "cheat" and just pick a word you think is fascinating.

Create a mind map with the word. Take the word as many places as you can. Take a branch of your mind map and use that as inspiration for your collection.

DESIGN BRIEF 6: MODERNIZING HISTORY

Many of us are inspired by specific people, whether it's their style, lifestyle, or personality. Select a historical figure and design a wardrobe for them as if they lived in modern times. You can bring in some elements of that person's lifetime, but this is not about costume design. Focus more on this person's life achievements, personality, and lifestyle. Create a customer profile around this historical figure, and how they would live modern day.

Example: Let's pretend Harriet Tubman lived in modern-day America. Harriet Tubman (1822-1913) was an escaped slave and political activist who made over a dozen missions to rescue slaves in the 1850s. During the Civil War, she worked for the Union Army and led a raid that liberated more than 700 slaves. Late in her life, she was active in the women's suffrage movement.

What kind of wardrobe would you build for her? How about an affordable, utilitarian everyday work wardrobe with lots of pockets? Easy-to-wear looks that include some day-to-night looks? How about making the whole collection feminine without being fussy, using machine washable fabrics made of natural fibers? What details from the time period can you bring to present day without creating a costume? Portraits show Tubman in blouses with beautiful pleating, tucking, shirring details; in big, long, simple coats over her period-dictated long skirts. Her neck was usually covered by detachable collars or scarves. Think about incorporating these elements without making it look like costume design.

DESIGN BRIEF 7: A TOURIST IN YOUR OWN CITY

Visit the places your town is famous for that you're too busy living life to visit.

If you find the architecture inspiring, select one to four pieces of architecture that interest you. Analyze line, shape, form, color, texture, patterns. Analyze the mood and attitude of the buildings and how they interact with people. Is it a cozy, welcoming space, or an awe-inspiring, grandiose presence? Translate your analysis into clothing design.

If you're designing a small collection (four to eight looks), choosing one style of architecture would make the most cohesive collection. If you're doing larger collections, you have more visual space to play with how different architecture styles can interact with each other.

Or hit a crowded area and go people watching. Take some notes or sketch some interesting characters. You don't have to pick the most stylish person—pick someone you think seems interesting. Create a fake life story for this person. Develop a collection inspired by this character.

One day I saw this incredible sight. This very petite, slightly hunched-over Asian grandma, wearing a massive, shiny, black, puffy, quilted short parka and a pair of what can only be described as flower-print pantaloons, was furiously riding a neon Huffy kid-size bicycle, not giving a single fluffernutter about the traffic. I fell in love immediately. In lieu of stalking her and asking her to adopt me and teach me her ways, I designed a collection inspired by her.

DESIGN BRIEF 8: DECONSTRUCT AND RECONSTRUCT

Buy three garments in a thrift store or pull three garments from your closet you'll never wear again. Take photos of them (front, back, side, detail close-ups) for your mood board. Drape the garments onto your dress form in new ways over and over again. Situate them upside down and/or inside out on the dress form. Open up some seams. Also try combining two or three garments into one garment. Drape, fold, pin, and photograph. Repeat over and over in new ways. Print out your photos and use these drape experiments as inspiration for your collection. You can draw on your photos and expand upon the design, or you can layer tracing paper on top of your photo and draw out the design through simplifying and adjusting the drape.

DESPERATELY SEEKING INSPIRATION

Here's a list of activities and places that might fire up some creative synapses.

- Visit different local museums and attend exhibitions not related to fashion. Many museums also have internet archives, video tours, and similar.

- Watch a movie, preferably a type of movie you don't usually see. Don't scroll on your phone. Re-costume the movie.

- Watch a TV show you've never seen before from a much older time and re-costume it as a modern show.

- Shop in stores you've never been to or are the opposite of your general tastes. Window shop for things you haven't been interested in before—random stuff like old clocks, military surplus, wigs, and party supplies.

- Spend some time in a fabric store and explore areas you often ignore.

- Visit stores that sell other clothes-making materials, in particular those you don't usually use, like bead shops, yarn shops, craft shops, corsetry supply shops.

- Visit a candy specialty shop, the kind with big clear buckets of cool-looking treats. Put together a bag full of colors and textures that appeal to you. Take pics before you eat them all.

- Explore nature. Go on a hike, go camping, maybe glamping instead, take a drive through the woods, ride a train, visit a park or garden.

- Pull out your markers or colored pencils and select two or three colors you hate. Add two to four more colors to create a well-rounded color story and design around these colors.

- Think about a serviceperson you meet in your regular life, like a fast-food restaurant employee or package delivery person. Redesign their uniforms, taking into consideration their job responsibilities, weather, and logos. And you know, you should make them look a little cooler.

- Go to your local bookstore (or shop online) and hit the bargain bin. There are always some oddities in the bargain bin. Buy something fun and offbeat. This is how I discovered one of my favorite books, *Extraordinary Chickens*.

- Take a class at a junior college, community art center, or university extension program. These classes tend to be inexpensive if you're not taking them for college credit. The class doesn't have to be fashion related to get your creative juices flowing.

- Listen to a new or old favorite album. Pick a song and design and costume a music video for it, even if it's music that usually doesn't use music videos, like opera or classical.

- Volunteer at a local event. Runway shows always need model dressers and other backstage help. Theater and opera productions always need a bit of help backstage or in wardrobe. Volunteer and get to know other people who enjoy making things. And the rush of events and shows can be very energizing and inspiring.

Write out your design direction for your current collection here. Refer back to this direction when you start feeling lost.

_____

_____

_____

_____

_____

_____

_____

_____

_____

_____

_____

_____

_____

_____

_____

_____

_____

_____

_____

_____

_____

_____

Start mindmapping here. Take notes on literally anything and everything loosely related to your initial inspiration. Go back to your design brief and answer those questions. Let your mind wander past the answers to those questions and just keep writing and doodling. There is no bad idea at this point.

Based off your best bits from your design direction and mindmapping, gather your inspiration images, whether it's your artist's paintings or photos of your thrifted garments. Compile your notes, doodles, and images here and start collaging. The goal is to make yourself look at your inspiration images in new and different ways to spark your creative gears.

Here's a list of possible techniques to get you started. Have fun!

• Make multiple copies of each picture. Cut them apart to focus on one section at a time.

• Blow up one or more of the above cut sections and add to the original picture to play with scale and layering.

• Take a cut-up section and lay out the multiples to play with repeats to start the design of potential prints. We'll talk more about designing prints in chapter 5, but for now, play around with some initial concepts.

• Layer a piece of tracing paper on top and trace out interesting elements. Play with those elements. Think about those elements as silhouettes for clothes, motifs for embellishments, and shapes for sections of clothes like collars and sleeves,

• Layer two of the above tracings to see how the elements merge together and sketch out the results.

• Redraw the art with your own hand and see how your own line quality changes the look.

• Trace a small section of the art image. Remove the art image and freehand draw more—extending, expanding, exploring.

And feel free to revisit these pages and add/edit to your heart's content.

These pages are also for collection planning notes. Think about the season you're designing for and how that will affect the kinds of clothes you're designing. Think about how many outfits, how many sweaters, how many pairs of jeans you need to design for this collection.

4
COLOR

Let's talk about color. What colors do you love?

_____

_____

What kinds? Neutrals? Brights?

_____

_____

What colors do you love so much you want to include them in all or most of your design work?

_____

_____

Other opinions on color usage?

_____

_____

_____

_____

_____

_____

_____

EXERCISE 1: ANALYZING COLOR STORIES

Complete this analysis for at least three collections from different brands.

Make a list of brands that you aspire to be compared to, brands that cater to a similar customer, have maybe a similar aesthetic vibe. Back when I was in fashion school, my teachers would ask us, if Nordstrom bought your stuff, which designers would you want to hang with? Which section of Nordstrom would you fit?

_____

_____

_____

_____

_____

_____

_____

_____

_____

_____

_____

_____

_____

_____

_____

From one of these brands, pick a fashion collection in which you admire the colors. Analyze the colors by answering the following questions. Analyzing color stories you like will help you understand _why_ you like the color stories specifically, so you can apply what you learn to your own color stories in the future.

How many colors are used versus neutrals? What is the proportion of colors to neutrals used? (These are two different questions. There could be a lot of bright colors and only two neutrals, but those two neutrals could be used for 75% of the looks.)

_____

_____

_____

_____

_____

_____

_____

_____

Let's talk about wearable versus pop colors. Even bright colors can be wearable. Red is bright but popular and wearable. Lime green, not so much. What's the balance of light versus dark colors? Wearable/classic versus pop colors?

_____

_____

_____

_____

_____

_____

_____

_____

Do you think the colors match the fabrics? Maybe chartreuse looks great in a luminous silk charmeuse but cheap in a coarse linen?

_____

_____

_____

_____

_____

_____

Do you think the colors suit the season? If not, what would you change to make the colors suit the season better?

_____

_____

_____

_____

_____

_____

What kind of mood does the color story create?

_____

_____

_____

_____

_____

_____

Do the colors elevate the designs or fight them?

This analysis is also about figuring out what you gravitate toward. What about this collection's color story do you like or not like? What would you change?

EXERCISE 2: ANALYZING A BRAND'S COLOR USAGE

Pick three to four fairly recent collections from one brand and analyze them, using the prompts from the previous exercise. Compare the answers throughout the collection and note all the common threads.

What are the colors the brand uses in every or almost every collection? These colors don't need to be identical; they can very similar, like how Simone Rocha always uses a light pink in each collection but not always the exact same pink. She also often uses olive drab of varying shades.

_____

_____

_____

_____

_____

Does the brand lean toward neutrals or colors? Wearable or pops? Light or dark? Most people associate The Row with neutrals, but they also love a pop or three of red in most collections. People also think of Rick Owens as being heavy on black and greys but his womenswear collections are often more colorful than you would think. He actually shows a lot of pinks.

_____

_____

_____

_____

_____

_____

Read reviews of the collections. Can you see the correlations between the designer's inspiration and the colors used? Do you think the colors work to express the mood the designer was going for?

EXERCISE 3: PLAYING WITH COLOR COMBINATIONS

It's important that you pick not only a couple of great colors that express your brand but also great companion colors. Colors actually look different depending on what other color you put next to it.

Design a garment that requires two or more colors via elements like color blocking, a print, significant embroideries or other embellishments, or screen-print graphics. Sketch it out twice or make copies. Pick one color for the main parts of the garment. Pick different colors for the secondary parts of the garment. Observe how the main color changes with what's next to it.

What "works" depends on the effect you're going for.

If you want the appliqué to pop, pick a contrasting color like your main color's complement.

If you want the embroidery or color blocking to create a more harmonious overall look, pick a color of similar value or temperature.

Moving into the next exercises, think about whether you want to create more harmonized looks or high-contrast looks.

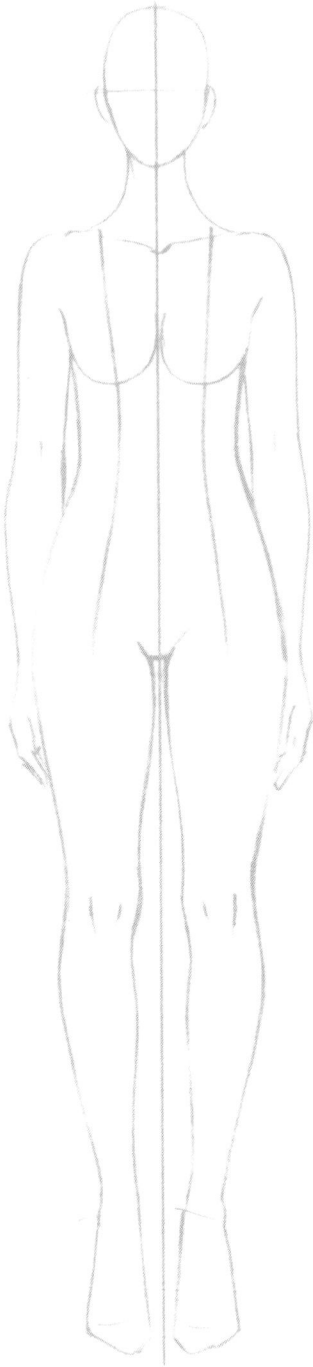

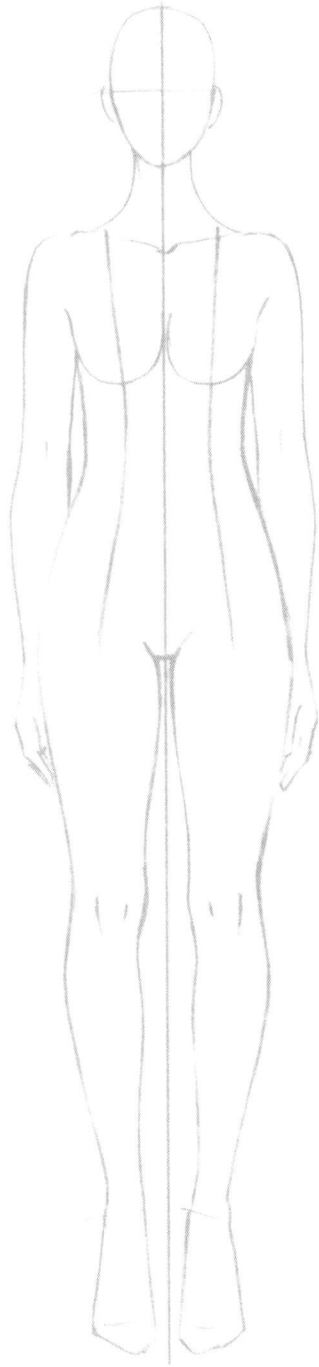

EXERCISE 4: COLORS FROM YOUR INSPIRATION

Refer back to your original inspiration to choose your colors. Do you have to? Yes, that's the whole point of inspiration. It's supposed to inspire all the visual aspects of your collection.

Look at the images and collages from your initial sketchbook and pull all your favorite colors. You can pick up to eight, but a few less is better. Use markers or paint to make big swatches of color. Colored pencils are slow to use but can be used in a pinch. Or you can take your sketchbook to a paint store and get paint chips. Cut your swatches into smaller squares. Do at least three groupings.

Choose your favorite grouping from the previous page and create two variations of that grouping. Even with this exploration, your color story should still look like it relates back to your original inspiration.

Original Grouping

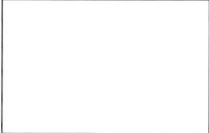

EXERCISE 5: COLOR PROPORTIONS

As you may have observed in earlier exercises, proportions of colors used in a collection can really change the overall mood and presentation. Using your favorite color story from the previous exercise, create three color proportion charts, showing how you plan to use each color.

Here are some variations you can work on: heavy on neutrals versus heavy on bright colors; heavy on light colors versus dark colors; as evenly spread out as possible; three main neutrals with a lot of small pops; heavy on warm colors versus cool colors.

Your best color story from
the previous exericse here:

5
PRINT DEVELOPMENT AND SURFACE DESIGN

The following pages describe some design exercises you can use to develop prints, patterns, surface design, and embellishments.

Take a sheet of tracing paper, go through your inspiration images, and trace a cool section you see—the more abstract the better. Tape it here. Scan into Photoshop and play around with this tracing. Distort it, flip it, twist it, granulate it. Have fun.

Travel through life with a scrap of tracing paper and a soft lead pencil or colored pencil. Do rubbings of any interesting texture you come across. Tape your scraps here. Translate the textures into patterns.

Take one of your inspiration images into Photoshop, remove all color, and increase the contrast until you get an abstract black-and-white design. Play.

Take photos of interesting negative shapes or pull negative shapes from your inspiration and play.

Spend a couple of hours absentmindedly making marks on paper. Look at your inspiration images for a while and then put them away. Play some music or watch a show that fits the vibe of your project.

Choose one of the prints you designed and overlap it with a classic pattern like polka dots, stripes, plaid, or check. Or you can layer two of the prints you developed.

EXPLORE PATTERN DIRECTIONS

The direction of the print affects the overall look.

You can have a one-direction pattern, where the pattern only looks "correct" in one direction. Your garment pattern pieces have to be cut in all one direction in order to look right.

You can have a two-direction pattern, where the pattern looks "correct" in two directions. You can cut the pattern in either direction.

You can have a four-direction pattern, which you can cut any which way, and it gives a really different look than a two-direction pattern.

one direction

two direction

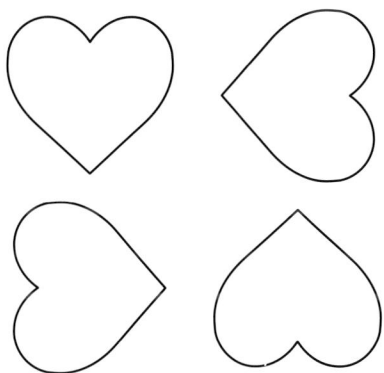

four direction

EXPLORE PATTERN REPEATS

Given the same design motif, you can create a lot of different looks with different repeats. Here are some common pattern repeats.

full drop/block

half drop

brick

diamond

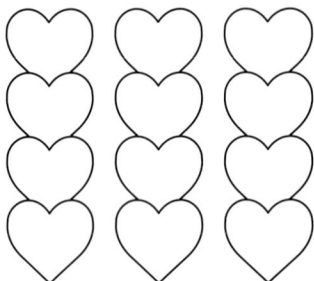

stripe

Then think about putting a direction and a repeat together.

half drop two direction

brick four direction

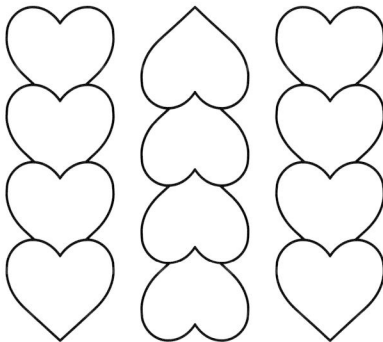

stripe two direction

EXPLORE PATTERN SCALE AND COLOR

Now that you have a design motif, a direction, and a repeat, you should think about the size of the pattern in relation to the body.

Use a figure template and layer the pattern onto the figure in Photoshop or Illustrator.

You can also have two prints that are based on the same base design. You can use the flower you designed and create a large-scale print and then create a ditsy print with itty-bitty versions of the same flower.

Use the following figure templates to explore scale and different colorways of your print(s).

Once you've developed a few prints you like, start applying colorways. Start with your color story and make combinations with those colors, depending on how many colors you need for your print to work.

You can also add some colors, but the bulk of your colors should remain your original color story and shades of those original colors. If your colors include red, brown, and orange, you can include a few different tints, shades, and tones of red, brown, and orange to flesh out your print while still staying true to your original color story.

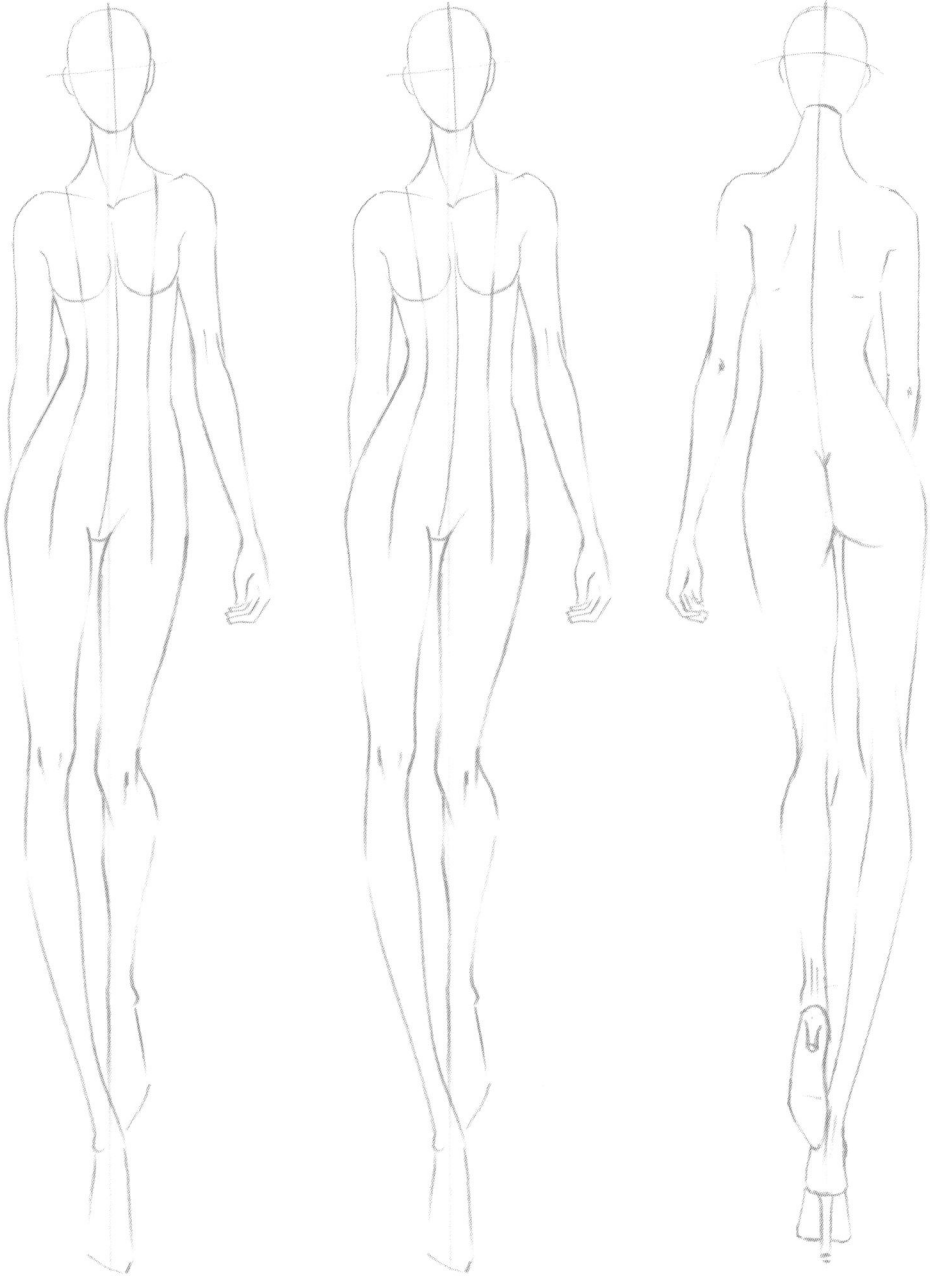

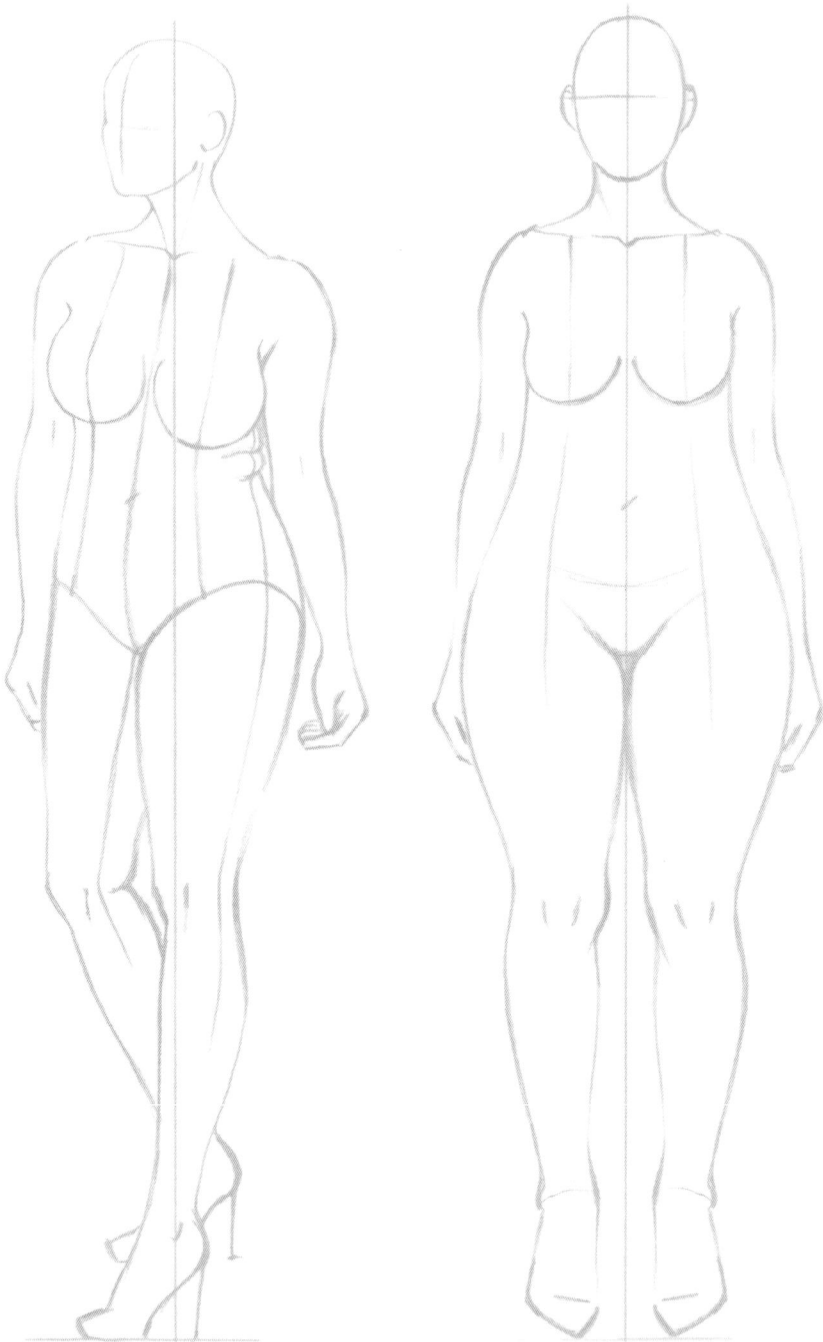

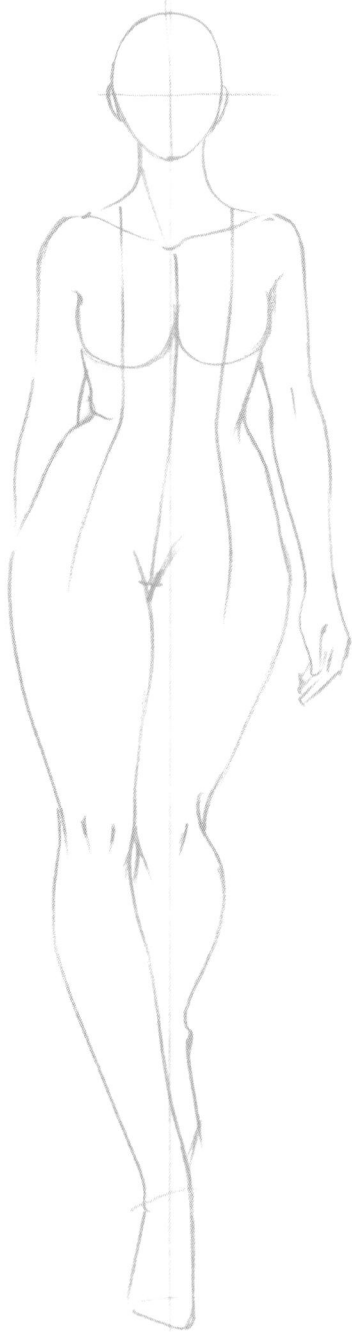

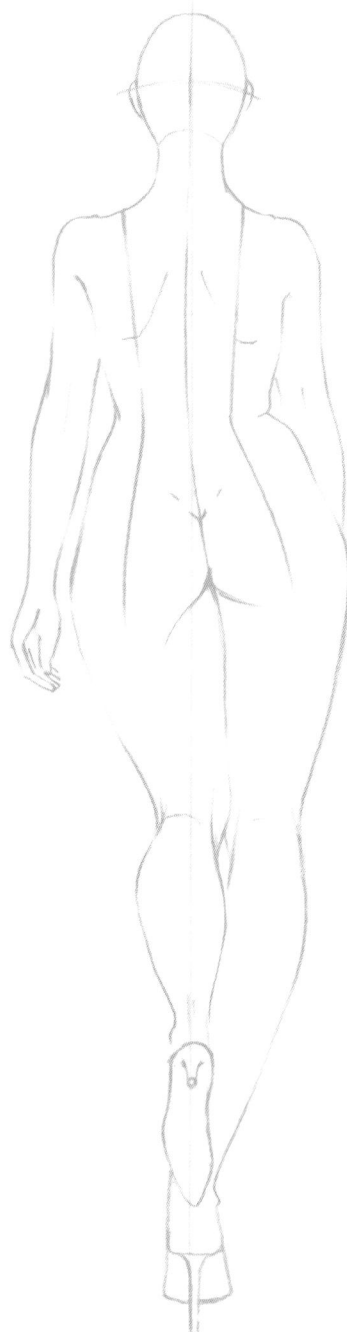

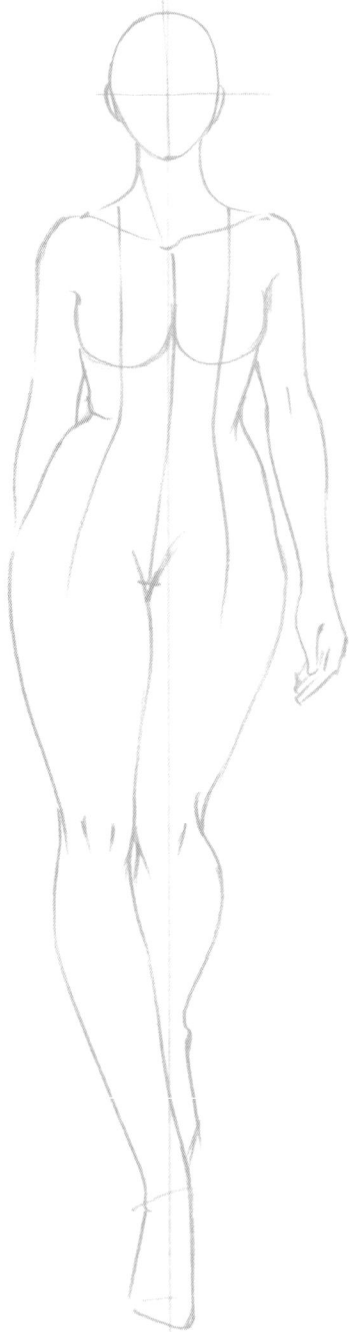

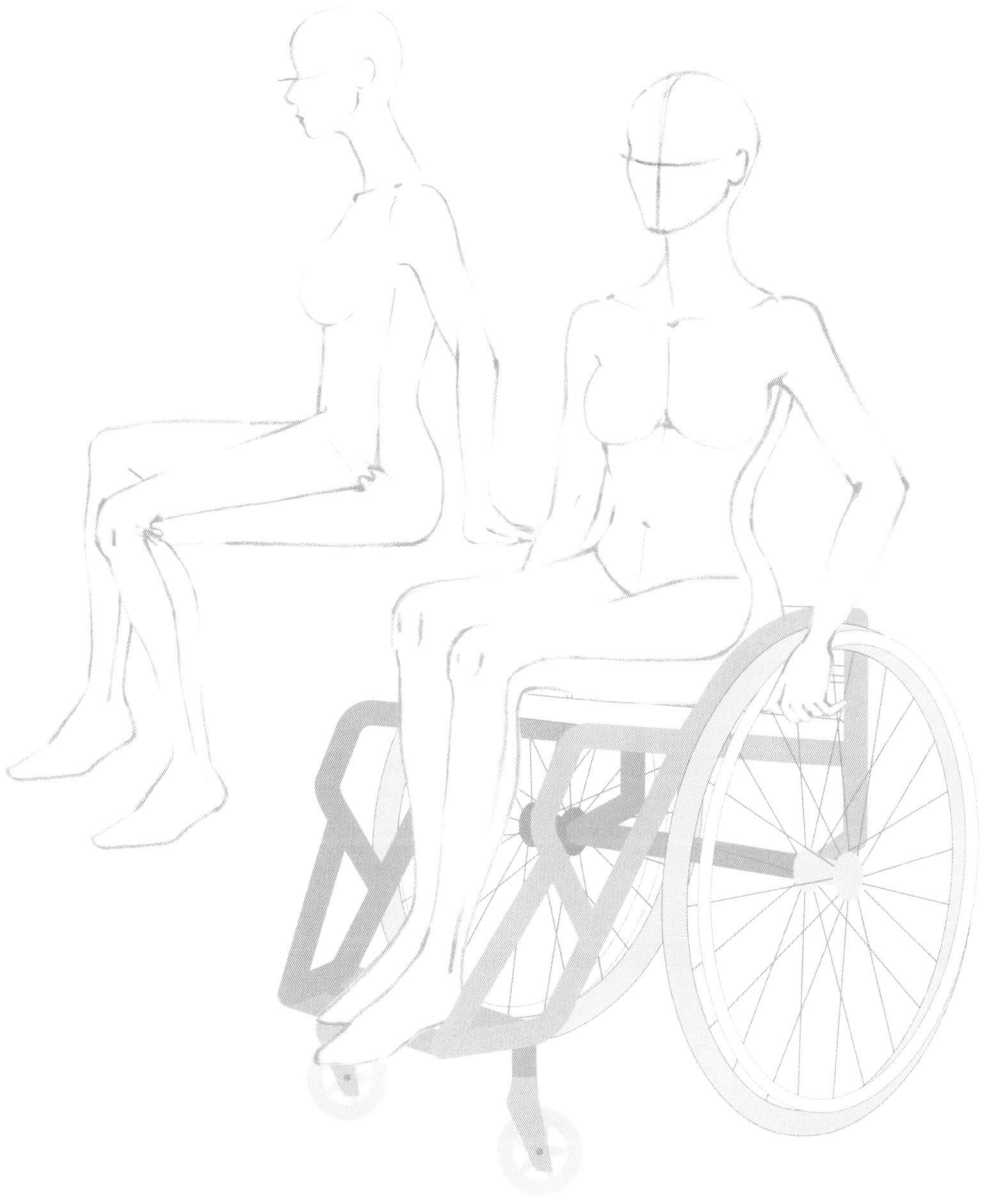

SPIN-OFF EMBELLISHMENTS

Pull elements from your finished print to create all kinds of other design elements for your garments. You can create:

- Graphics for screen-prints, appliqués, embroideries, beaded designs, patches

- Debossings or embossings

- A three-dimensional print, such as turning a flower print into fabric flowers

- A quilting pattern, by simplifying the print design

- Decorative stitches like smocking, using the print design for pattern inspiration

- Layers that build on the above ideas, such as beading a quilted fabric or sewing flowers onto a flower print

Use these blank pages to sketch out some ideas.

6
FABRIC

In a documentary about his work, Dries Van Noten said, "I always start with the fabric."

Nothing beats touching real fabrics when trying to learn fabrics. You can read fabric books with swatches or pictures of fabrics. You can buy a swatch book with the swatches labeled.

Something I recommend to everyone is to hit a fabric store and read the info on the ends of the rolls and feel the fabrics. Pull some out, pick it up with two fingers to see if the fabric drapes smoothly or is stiff and crinkly. Feel the surface.

Test for give/stretch. Does it stretch along the selvedge, along the cross grain, and/or the bias? Is this because there's a percentage of spandex in the fabric or because it's a loose weave or knit?

Compare polyester chiffons, taffetas, and satins side by side with silk chiffons and satins. Polyesters tend to be shinier, while silks are more softly luminous. Polyesters tend to be stiffer in drape.

Check out the cut edge. Does it fray/unravel easily? Don't pull too many yarns out. That's just damaging product that doesn't belong to you.

Think about what kinds of things you can make with the fabric. Is it heavy enough for coats? Or great for slinky evening gowns?

By the way, the right side of the fabric is whatever side you want to use. Most fabrics have an obvious right side, like prints, velvet, and anything shiny. Otherwise, always swatch the fabric for your swatch card, pattern card, and tech packs with a special note on which side you're using for the right side. With some fabrics, this is especially important. Crepe-backed satin can just as easily be satin-backed crepe.

ANALYZING FABRIC STORIES

Pick a fashion collection in which you admire the fabrics. For best results, choose a collection that's the second most recent so you can examine the collection both on the runway and in stores. Don't pick huge brands who put eighty looks on the runway each season. Their fabric usage is not relatable to you right now. Analyze the fabrics and put them in categories. Answer the questions below to help you in your analysis, but also take notes on anything of special interest to you.

First check out the collection on the runway. How many looks are in the collection? How many bottomweights are being used? How many topweights? How many dressweights or novelties? Identify as many as you can, even if your notes read, "very soft-looking fuzzy knit?" or "white suiting that's a little shiny." You'll learn more as you study, but quite frankly, the best way to identify fabrics is to look at them up close and touch them. Don't feel bad if you can't precisely tell what something is from a runway photo. And you can also tell your fabric sales rep you're looking for suiting for blazers that's a little bit shiny.

How many colors does each fabric come in?

_____

_____

_____

_____

Are any fabrics used in an unexpected way? What do I mean? Anything that makes you think, "Hey, that was unexpected. I didn't know you could/should/were able to do that!"

_____

_____

_____

_____

Do any fabrics show special techniques such as laser cutting, all-over embroideries, beading, or special finishes? Describe as best you can, even if you don't know the precise techniques or what they're called.

_____

_____

_____

_____

What is the ratio of special developed/embellished fabrics to plain/simple/right-off-the-roll fabrics being used?

_____

_____

_____

_____

Next, look for the collection in stores. Look at the brand's website, look them up under the Google Shopping tab to find where else they are selling, and look up those listings. You will find more information on colors available and fiber content. If possible, try to find some pieces in stores and feel the fabrics. Keep adding what you learn to the questions above.

ANALYZING A BRAND'S FABRIC USAGE

Pick three recent collections all from one brand and analyze them like the previous exercise. Make note of fabrics used frequently throughout the collections, again even if you can only identify it as "slightly shiny suiting." Maybe you will find they consistently use this SSS.

Remember to pick a smaller brand that produces smaller collections. These exercises can get unwieldly with too many looks.

Do these exercises with different brands that you admire, that you consider your competition, to get a feel for a framework of fabric usage. This is helpful too if you decide to start a brand in a single garment category, like knit sweaters or jackets.

THINGS TO THINK ABOUT WHILE PICKING YOUR FABRICS

Pull textures from your inspiration images.

Make notes on what kinds of garments you're designing and what season you're designing. If you're doing coats, swatch a few options. If you know you want to do blouses, think about what a good winter blouse fabric would be versus a summer blouse fabric. Note what your customer loves and hates to wear.

_____

_____

_____

_____

_____

Also note which fabrics get a print and which fabrics get which colors. I'm probably not going to print a wool Melton coat fabric, as the fuzzy texture would interrupt the print, but I could possibly print a silk charmeuse for my dresses.

_____

_____

_____

_____

_____

Every single garment you design should be made available in multiple colorways, except possibly a very special novelty, like an all-over beading. You're not going to pour all that time, money, and effort into the product development of a jacket just for it not to sell because no one liked that shade of green you picked. Also offer it in a neutral like black or white, and a more popular brighter color like red or pink. Of course, what works depends on the garment. Many people like pink tops but pink pants are more niche. When you shop for fabrics, make sure they come in all the colors you need.

Brands have a lot of other considerations in choosing fabrics such as cost, country of origin (shipping logistics and taxes), MOQ (minimum order quantities), and customization options. Make sure you address these concerns with your fabric sales reps.

LAYERING AND COMBINING FABRICS

Not every fabric needs to stand alone. Think about how you can layer fabrics for either structural reasons or purely aesthetic reasons.

Underlining is not the same thing as lining. When you line a coat, you make the coat shell (outside fabric) out of one fabric, and then you line the inside of the coat with a different fabric. When you draft a pattern for this coat, the pattern pieces are all different.

When you underline a coat, you cut out the same pattern pieces of two different fabrics and stitch them together so the two layers function as one piece of fabric. And then the coat is sewn together and can even require a separate lining.

Think about making a lace coat. Most laces don't have enough structure and warmth to make a proper coat, but you could underline the coat with a more suitable coat material. Or you could layer the lace over organza to give a blouse more structure and make the overall look less sheer.

You can also think about underlining purely for the look. Whatever coat fabric you layer under the lace will affect the overall look. You don't have to stop there. You could stitch through both layers with a contrast thread that picks up the color of the coat fabric and highlights the shape of the flowers in the lace.

You could layer tulle on top of wool suiting, scrunching the tulle strategically. You could layer net over French terry, stitching the two together with little bar tacks. You could cut up a fabric and apply it to another fabric, like stitching leather strips onto denim.

Consider how to create your own fabric by knitting or weaving something other than threads or yarn, such as ribbon, elastics, zippers, bungee cords, leather strips, zip ties, wires, or strands of candy.

Scribble down some ideas to explore here.

Once you've done some studying, a lot of design research, some mindmapping, and a bit of messing around, it's time to buckle down and make some decisions. Use the following swatch card pages to track your fabrics. Make as many copies as you need.

fabric name: _____
fiber content: _____
description: _____
_____
width: _____
vendor: _____
price & date: _____
colors: _____
notes: _____
_____
_____
_____

fabric name: _____
fiber content: _____
description: _____
_____
width: _____
vendor: _____
price & date: _____
colors: _____
notes: _____
_____
_____
_____

fabric name: _____
fiber content: _____
description: _____
_____
width: _____
vendor: _____
price & date: _____
colors: _____
notes: _____
_____
_____
_____

fabric name: _____
fiber content: _____
description: _____
_____
width: _____
vendor: _____
price & date: _____
colors: _____
notes: _____
_____
_____

fabric name: _____
fiber content: _____
description: _____
_____
width: _____
vendor: _____
price & date: _____
colors: _____
notes: _____
_____
_____

fabric name: _____
fiber content: _____
description: _____
_____
width: _____
vendor: _____
price & date: _____
colors: _____
notes: _____
_____
_____

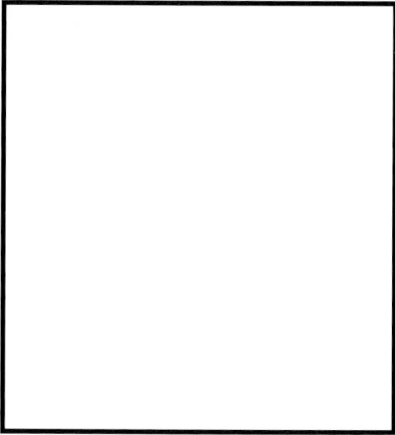

fabric name:
fiber content:
description:

width:
vendor:
price & date:
colors:
notes:

fabric name:
fiber content:
description:

width:
vendor:
price & date:
colors:
notes:

fabric name:
fiber content:
description:

width:
vendor:
price & date:
colors:
notes:

7

SHAPES AND SILHOUETTES

IS IT TIME TO SKETCH YET?

Yes! Are you excited? Gold stars for every student who patiently slogged through six chapters without skipping ahead.

Set up your workspace! Have your inspiration images, colors, fabrics, and prints in front of you so you are designing with these elements constantly reminding your brain. I don't know about you but I'm a little bit of an "out of sight, out of mind" sort of person, so I find this design board or sketchbook very helpful.

Have fun. Brainstorm, jot everything down, even if it's a section of a garment. Refer back to your sketchbook development for ideas on shapes to use. Use a figure template or flat template for efficiency. Designers don't have time to resketch the whole body every time they have a good idea. Using templates helps you work on consistent proportions in relation to the body, in relation to other designs you sketch, in relation to other parts of the garment.

Make plenty of photocopies of the figure and flats templates on the following pages (or download then at rockynook.com/fashionschool, or scan them into your drawing software of choice).

In this chapter, I have also included design exercises to explore shape. Even if these exercises don't relate exactly to your current project, they can get your creative juices flowing far faster than staring at a blank piece of paper.

DESIGN EXERCISES TO EXPLORE SHAPE

Is every design exercise for every designer? No, which is why there are so many. Do I think I'm a genius and you should try each and every one at least once? Maybe.

Refer to your sketchbook and isolate shapes and lines that you liked from your inspiration images. Use them to build your silhouettes and interior shapes. Use the figure templates in the following pages to explore the exercises below.

- Create and draw out an element. This element can be anything: a heart, a bow, a constellation of stars. Design garments incorporating that element (1) in the silhouette; (2) repeating the element in a smaller scale within the garment; and (3) scaled down very small and used as an embellishment. This is a great time to play with a motif you're considering for a house code. What's a motif that's important to you?

- Cut up random shapes out of paper or fabric in your color story colors. Use shapes found in your inspiration images. Paste them onto your figure templates. Develop, expand, elaborate.

- Sketch a flat of a garment, scan it into Photoshop, and use the transform tool to stretch, compress, and twist this design or sections of this design. Keep and print the best designs. Sketch on top of the printout to expand upon, elaborate, and finish the design.

- Fold up a piece of paper. You can choose to be absolutely random or fold a precise origami form. Perhaps the origami form refers back to your original inspiration. Open the paper and use the fold lines as inspiration for seam lines.

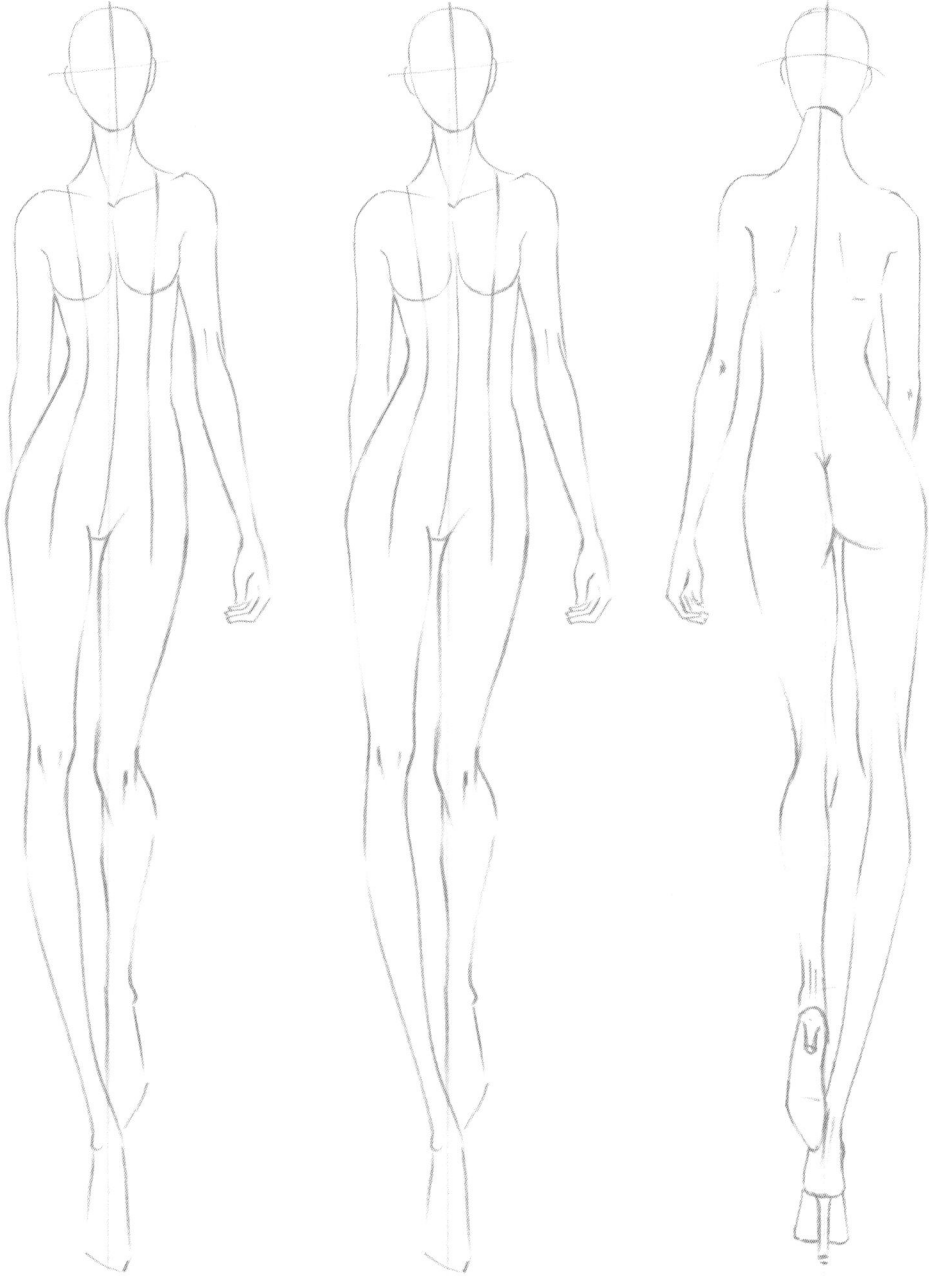

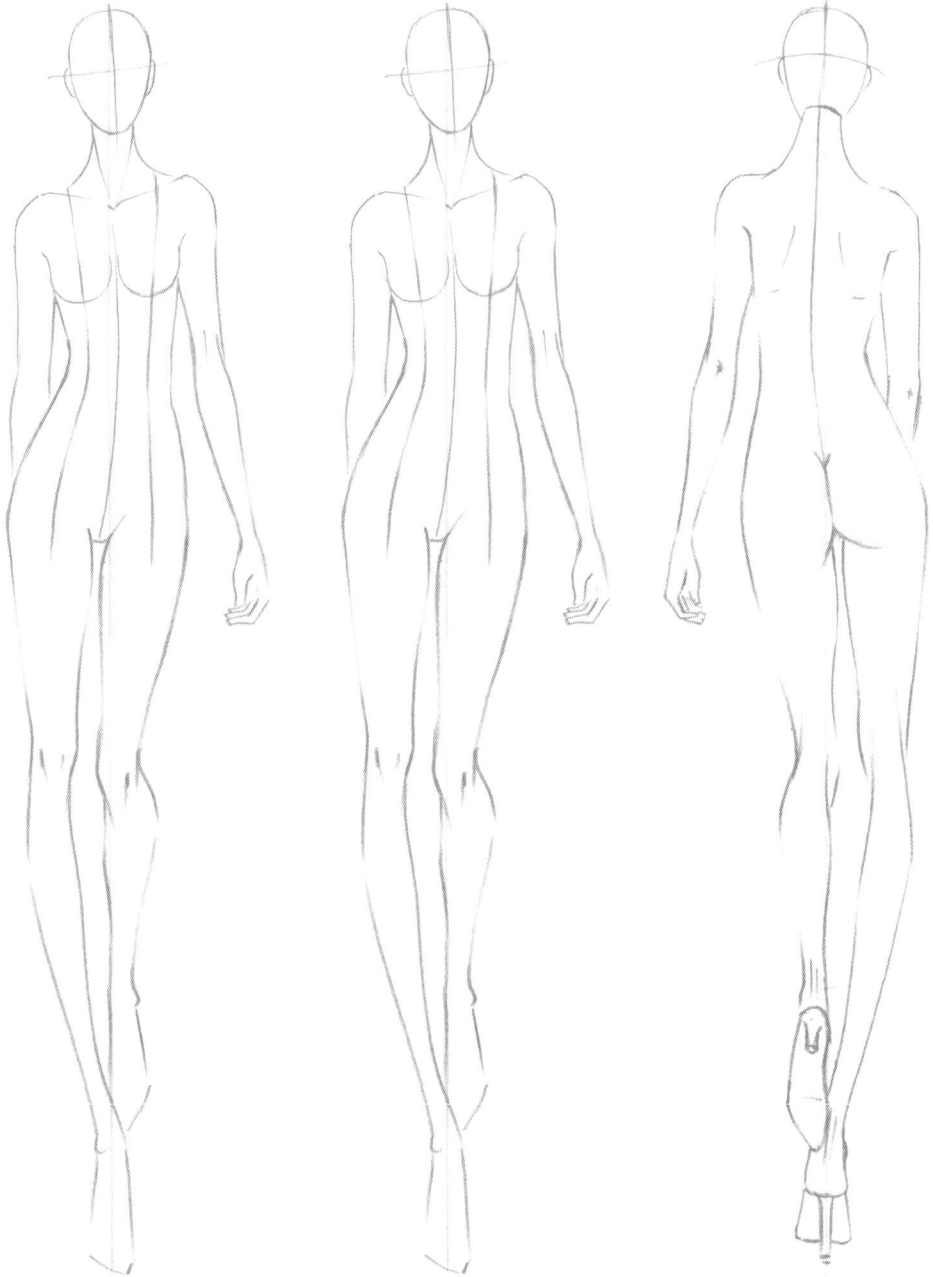

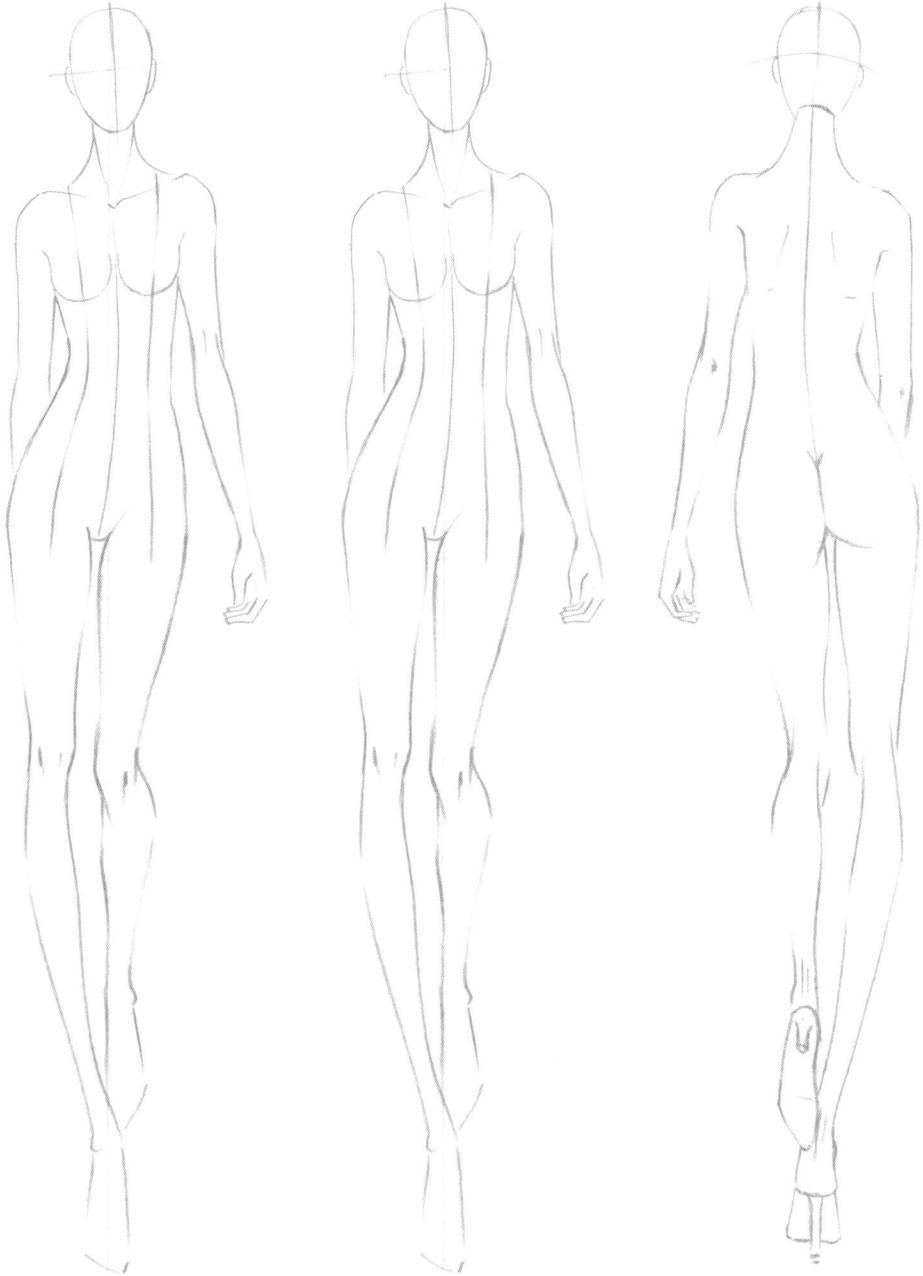

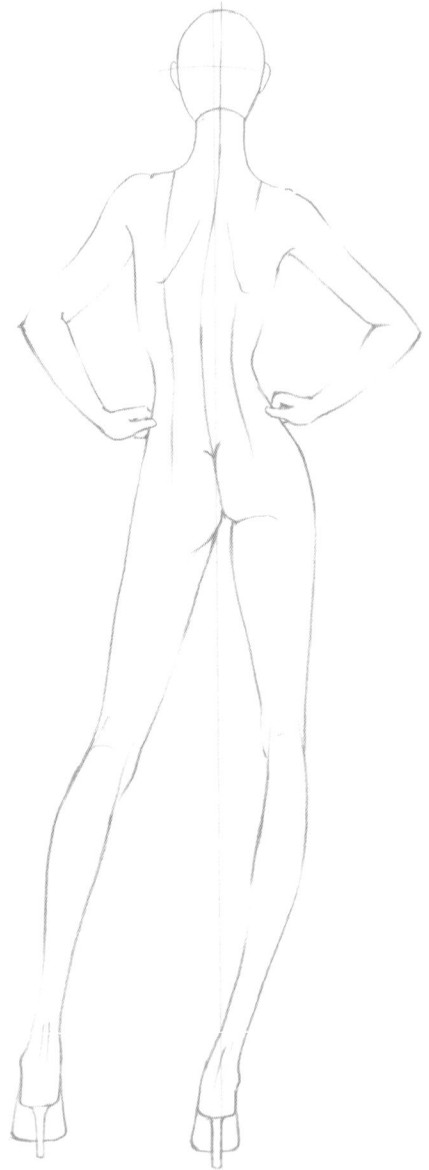

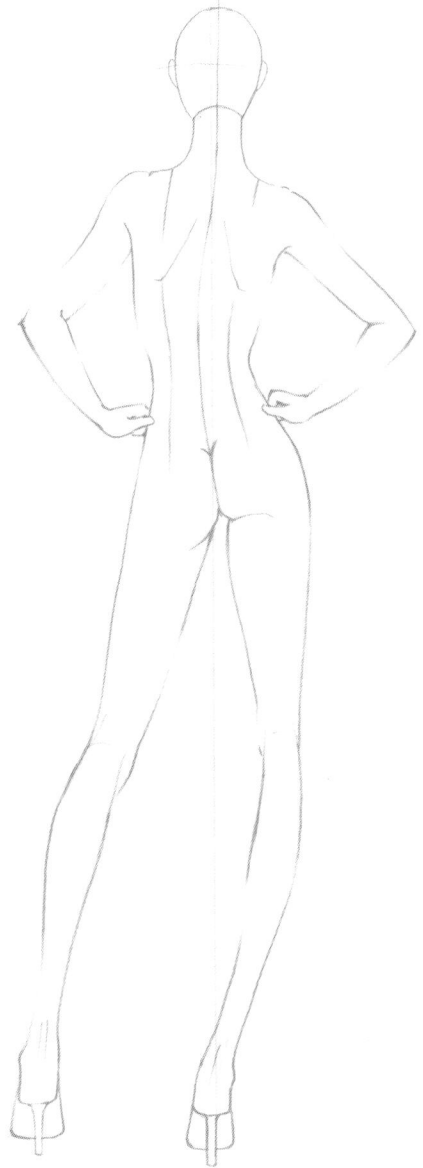

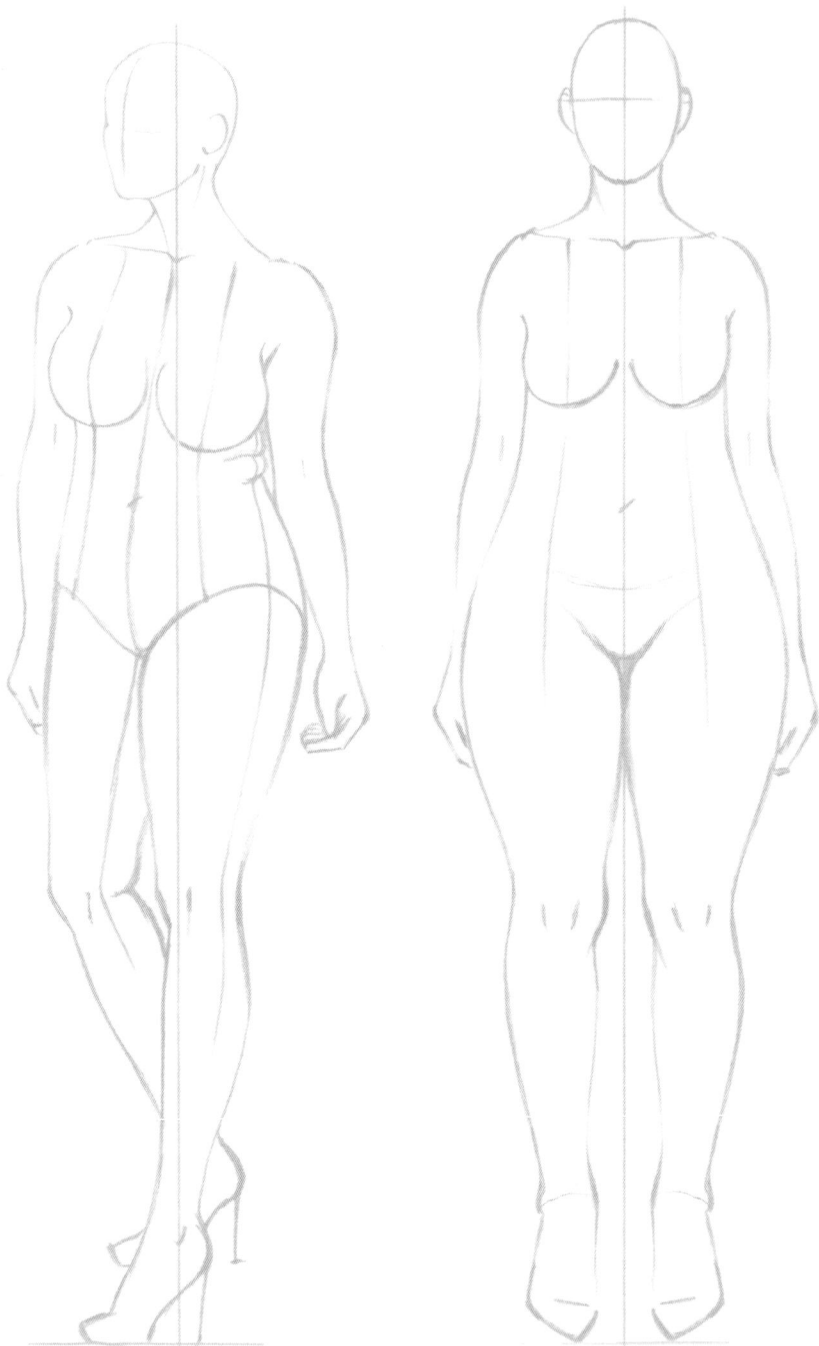

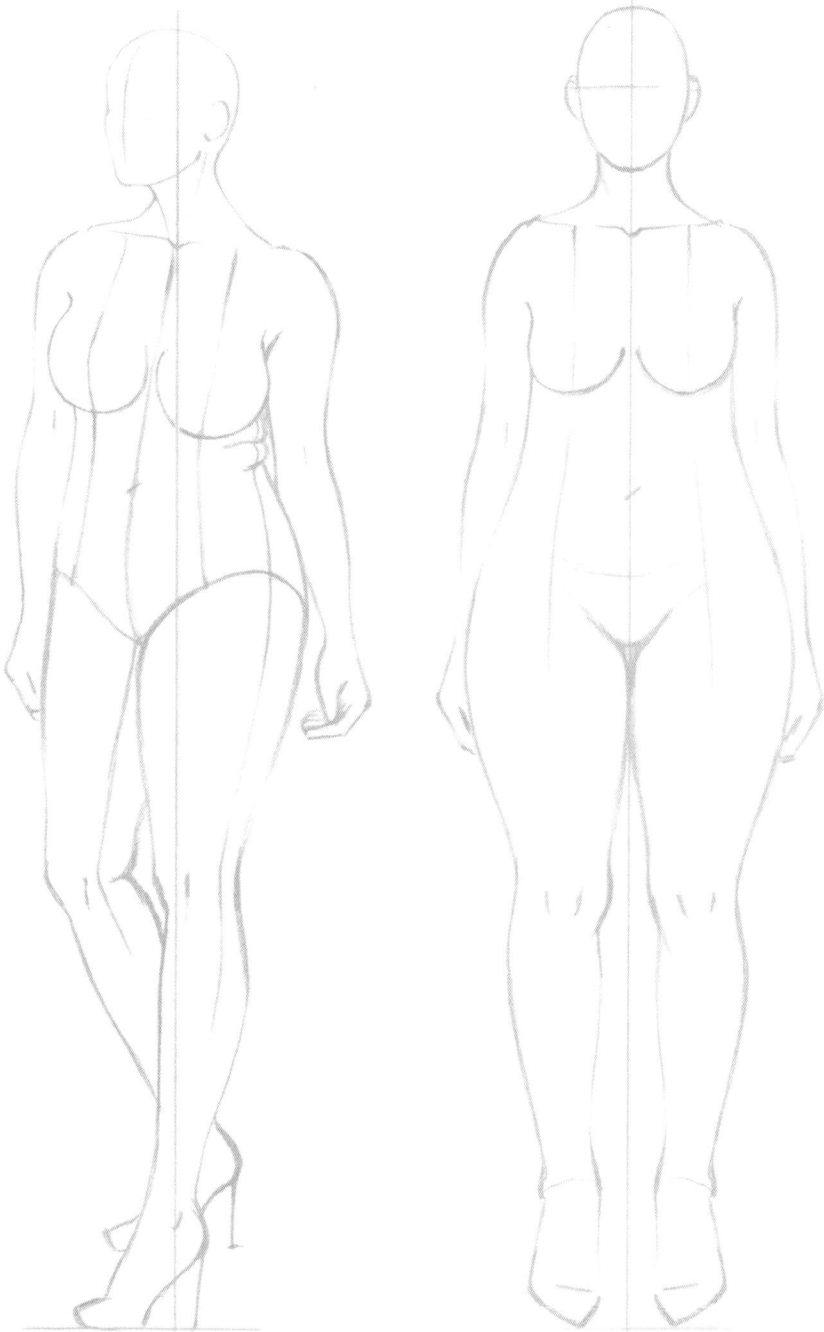

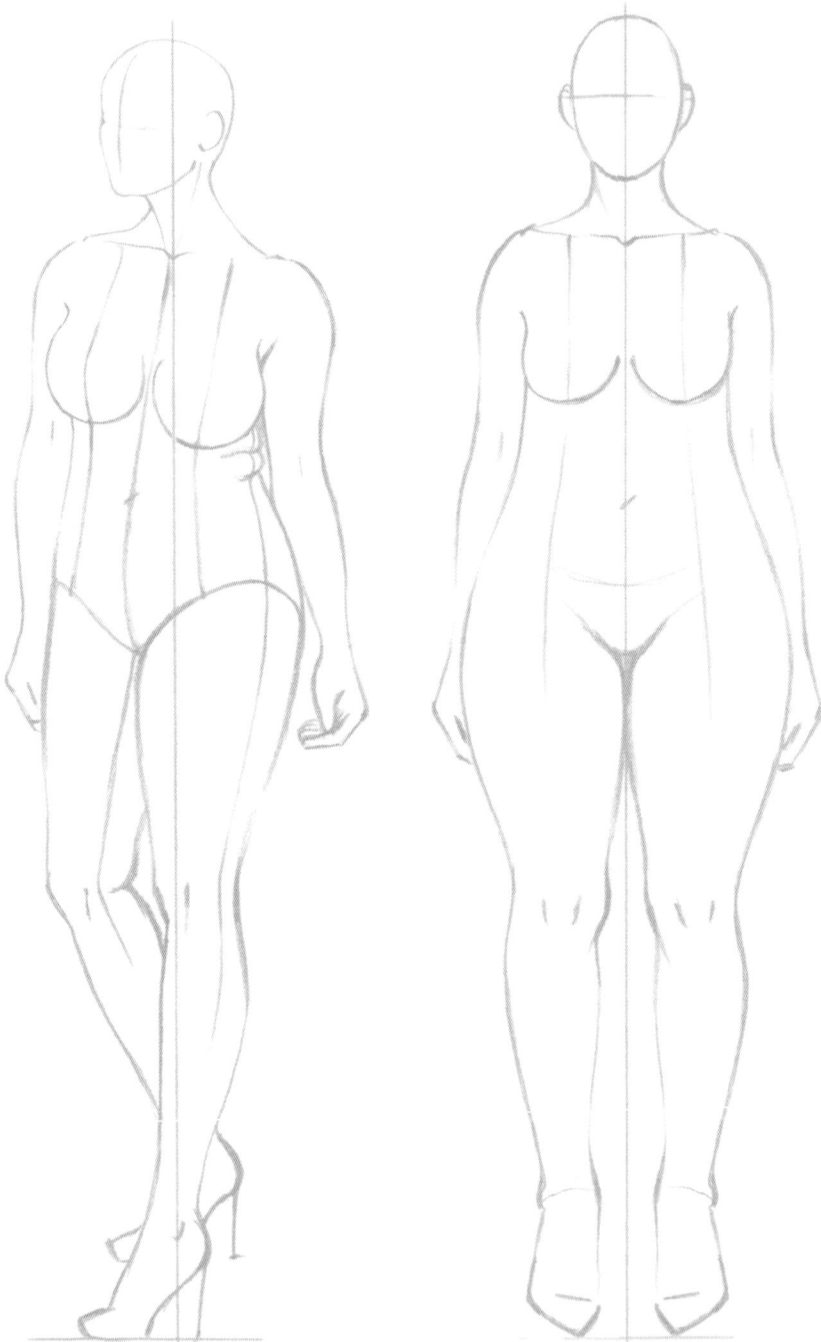

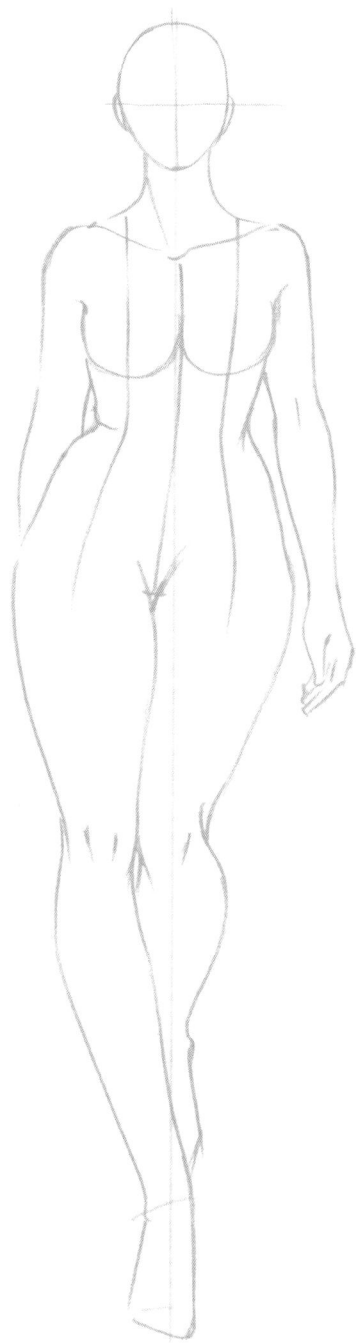

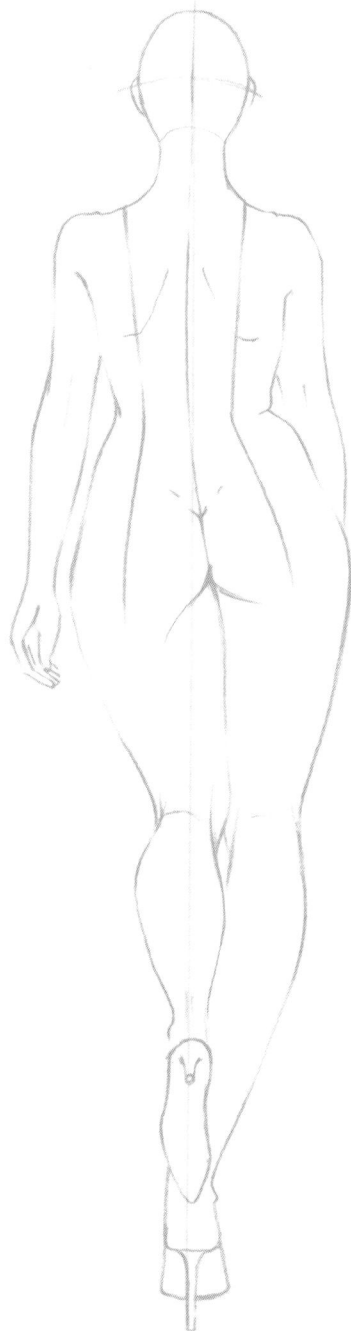

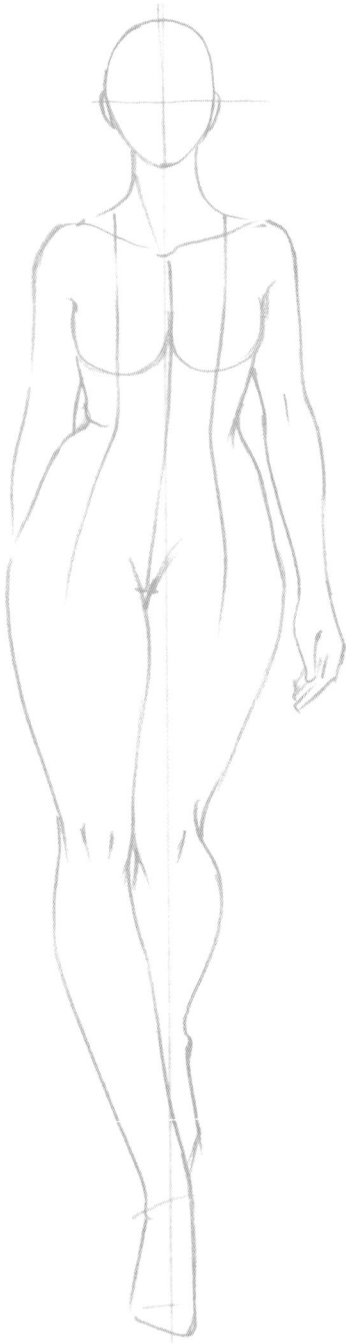

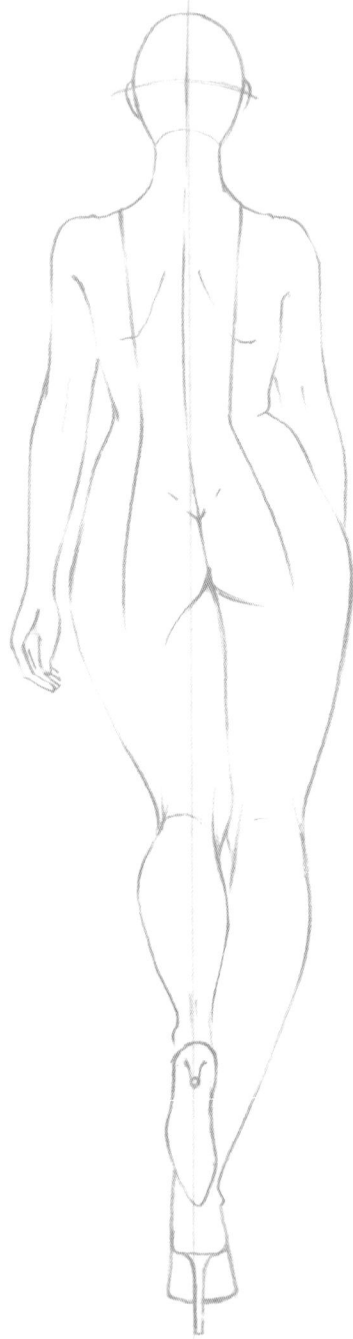

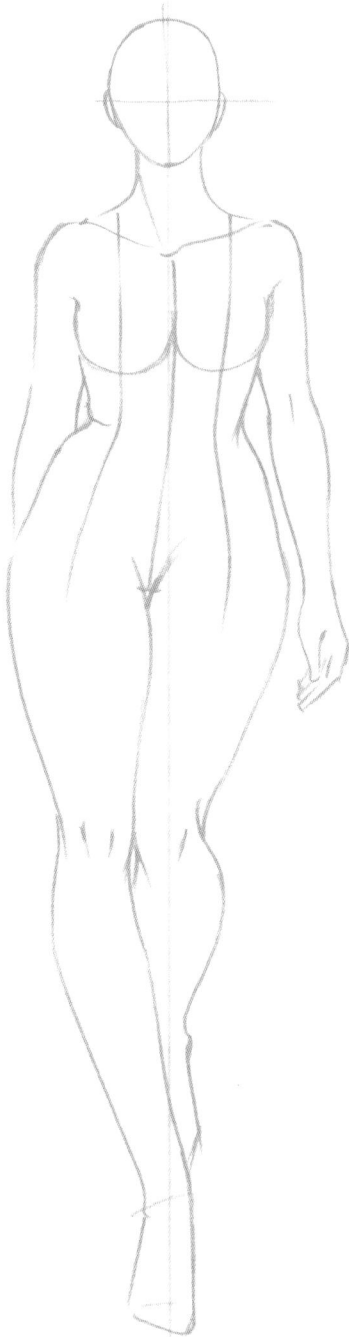

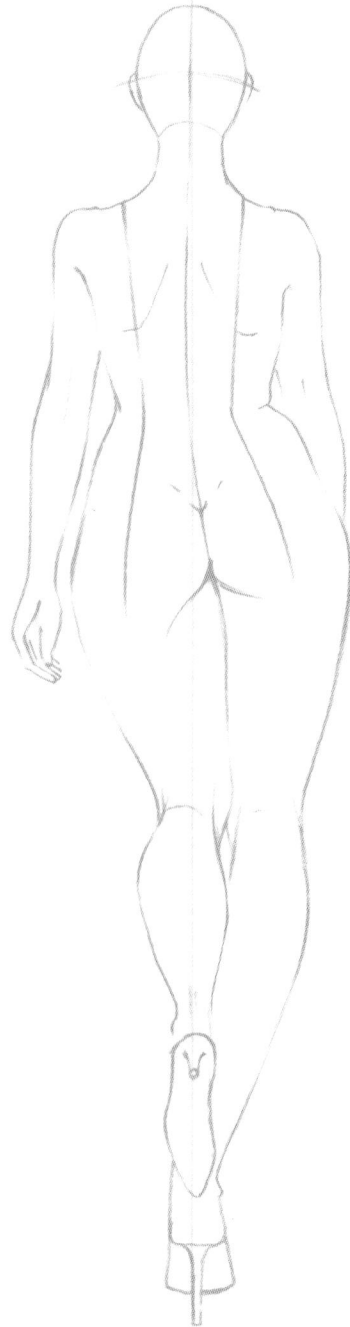

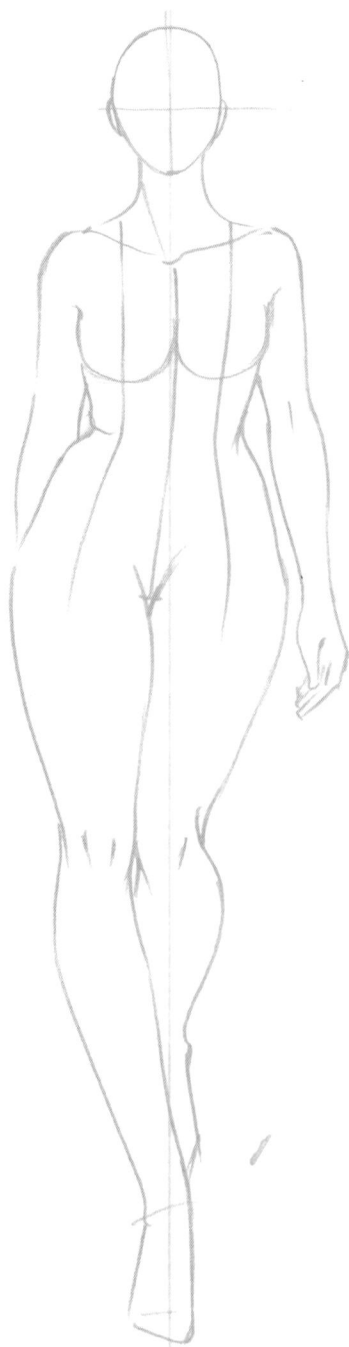

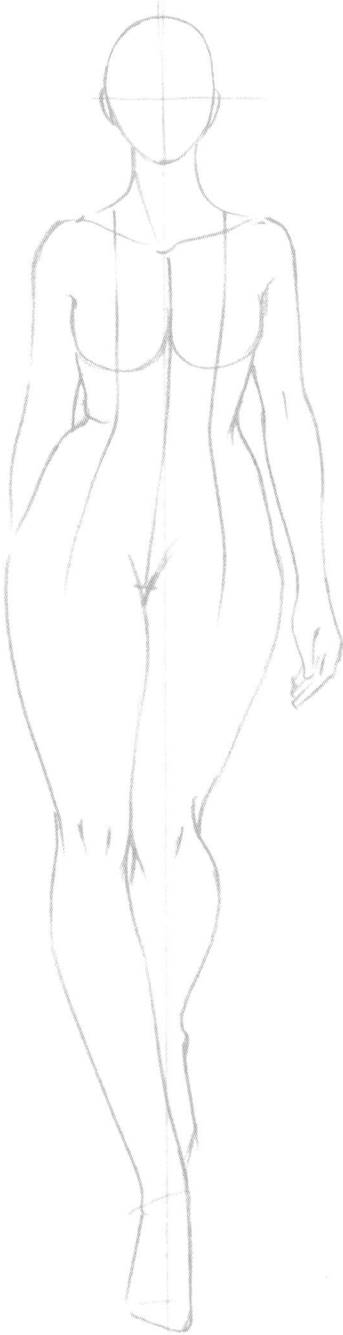

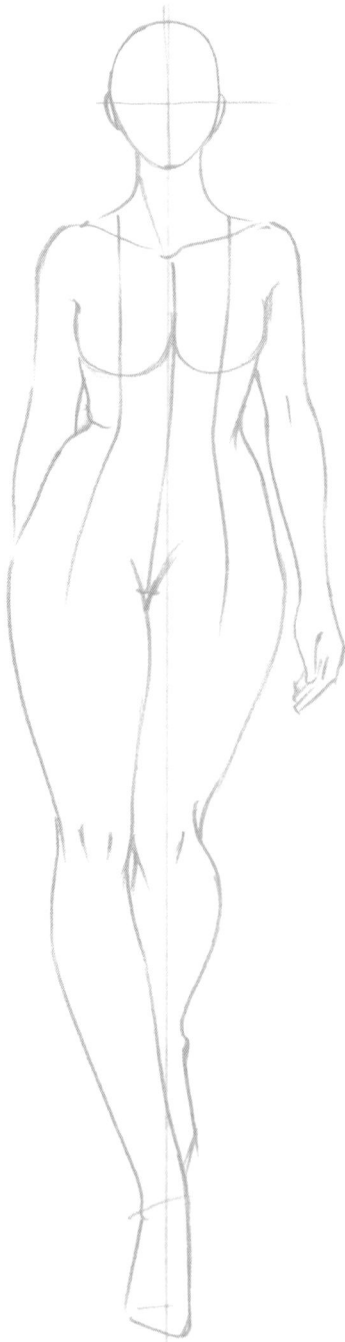

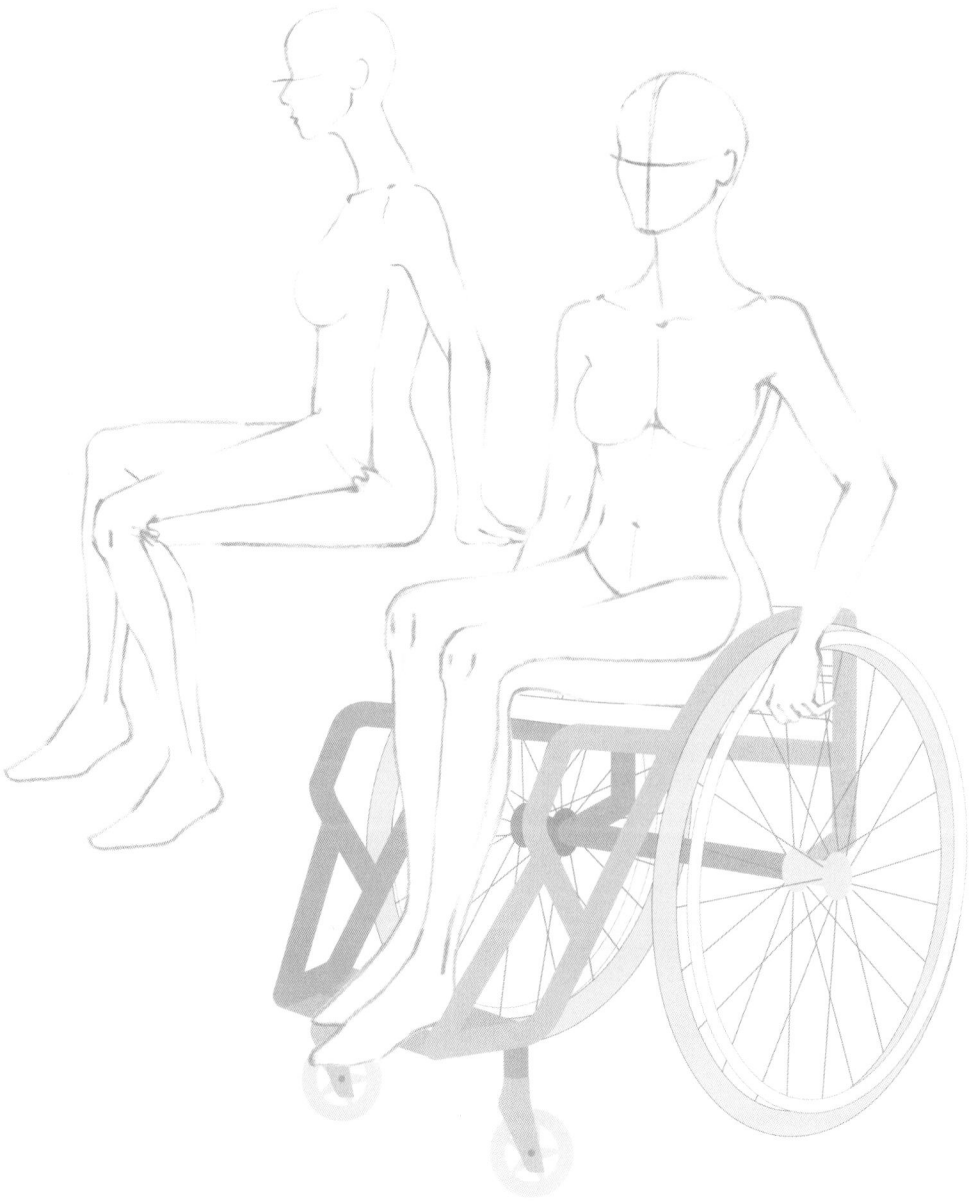

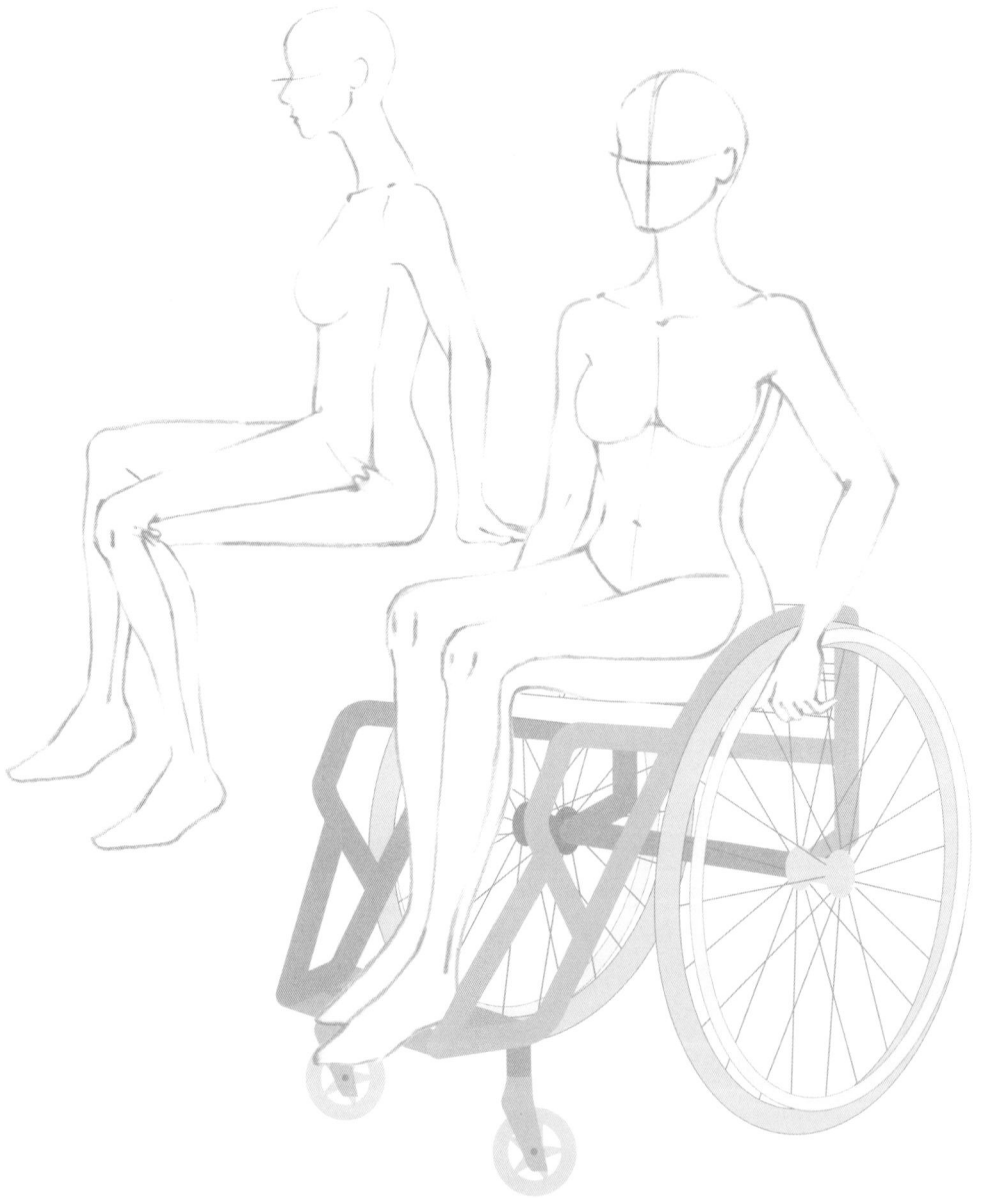

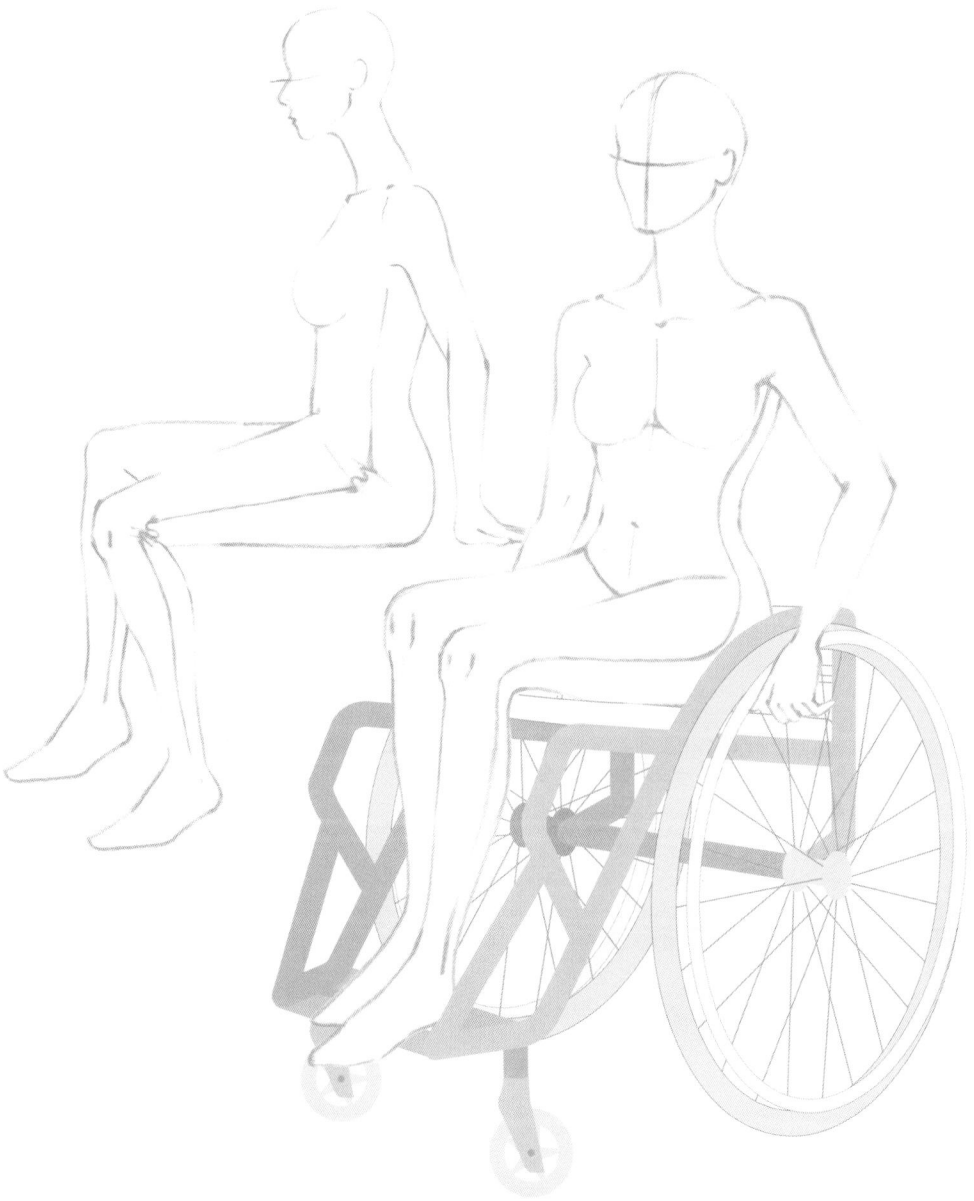

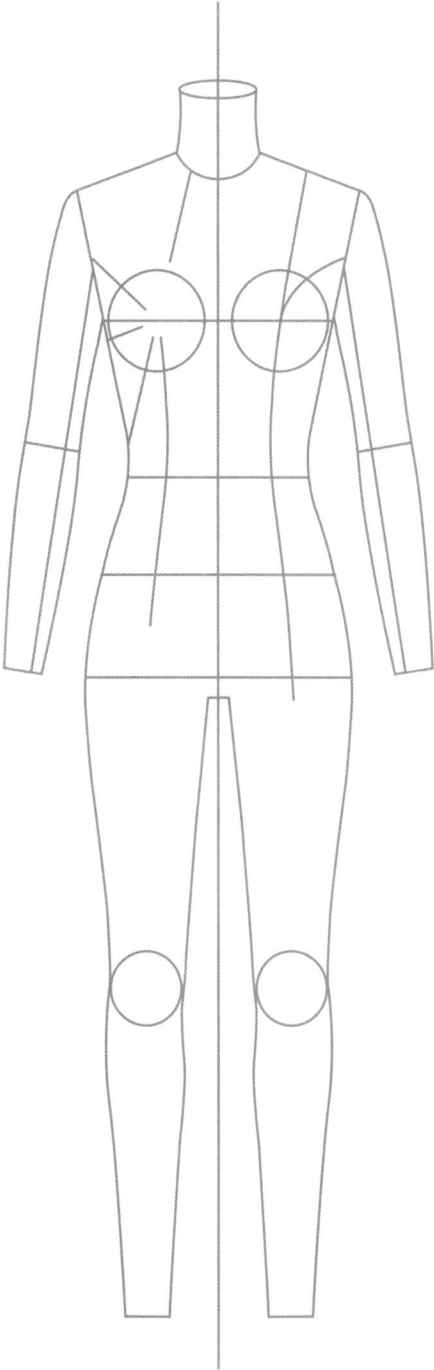

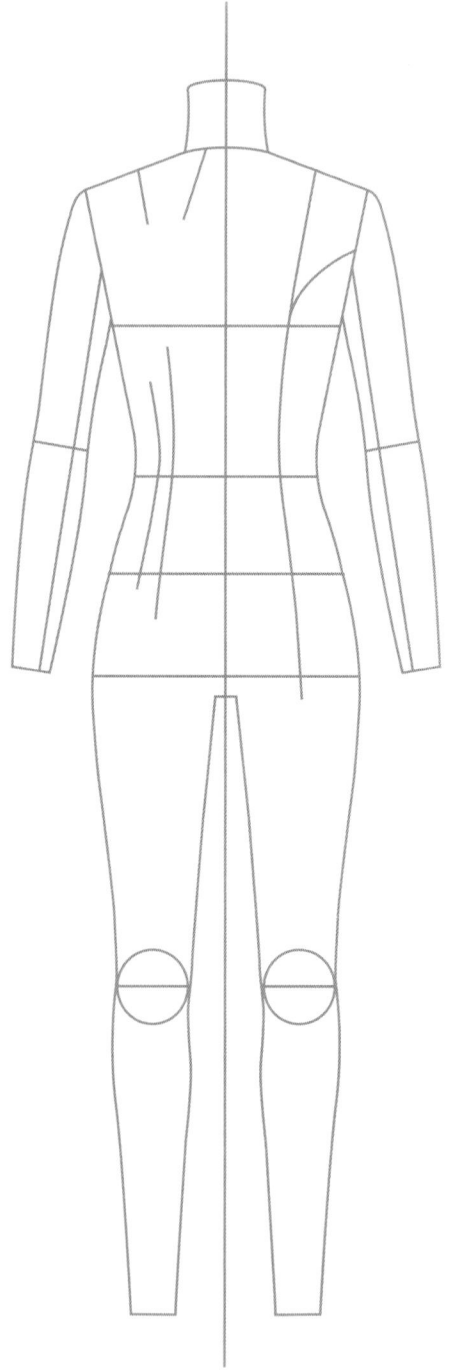

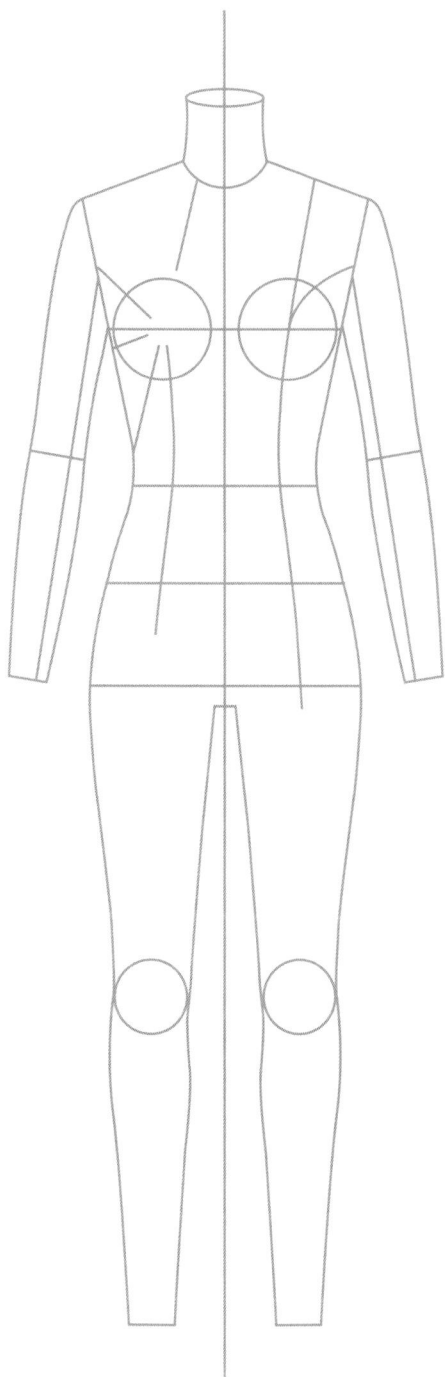

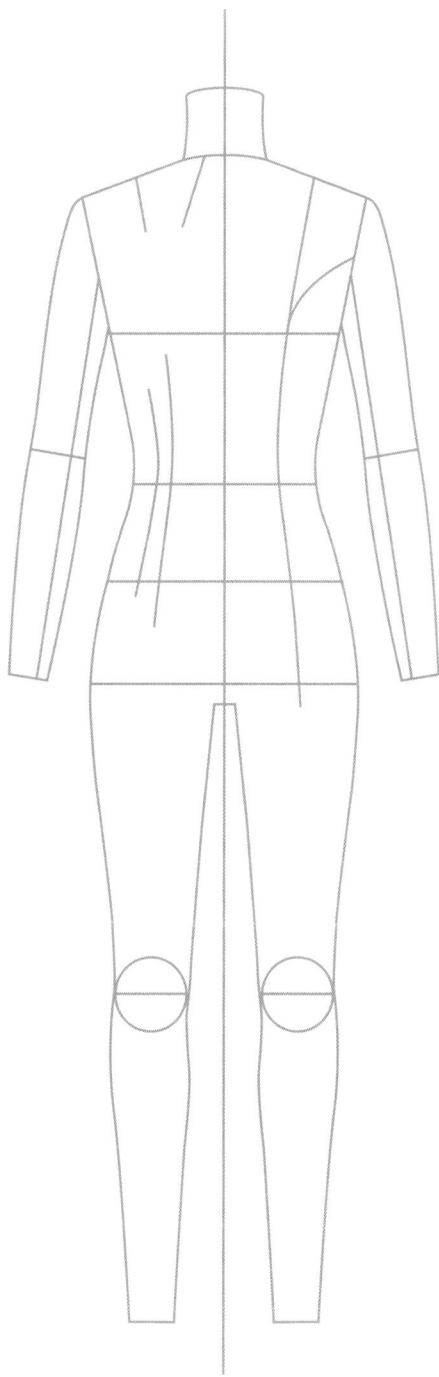

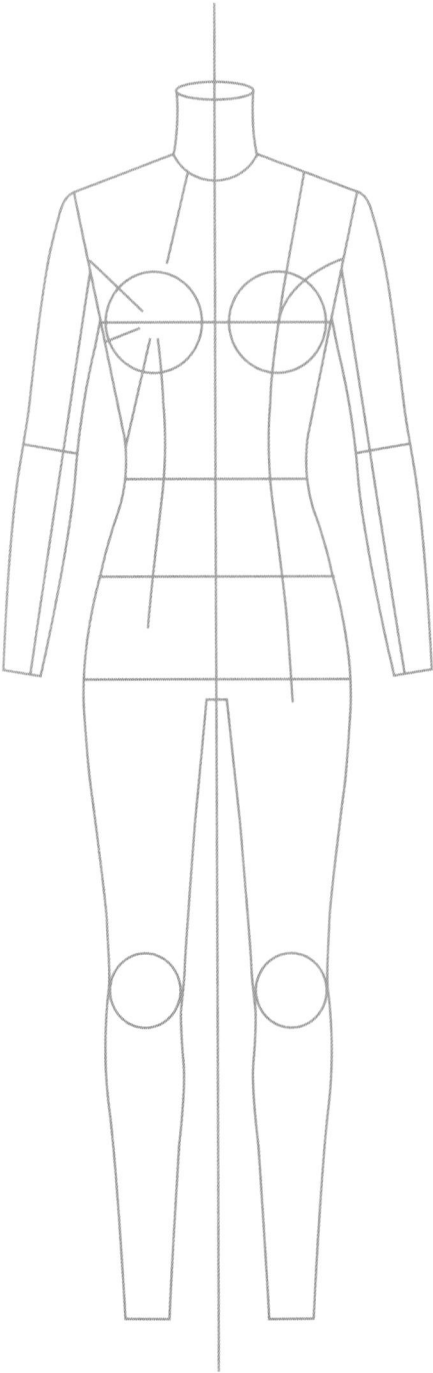

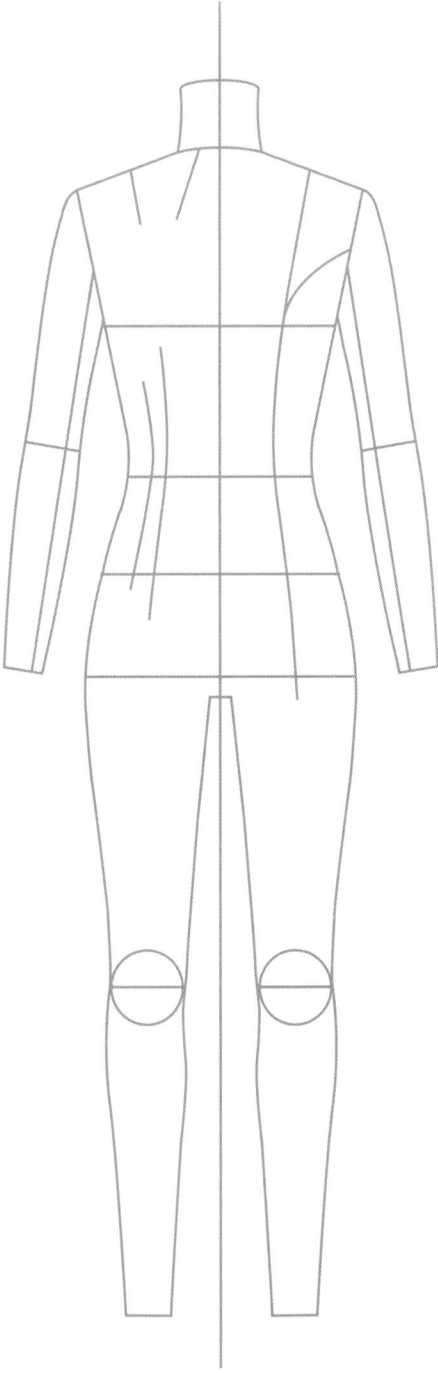

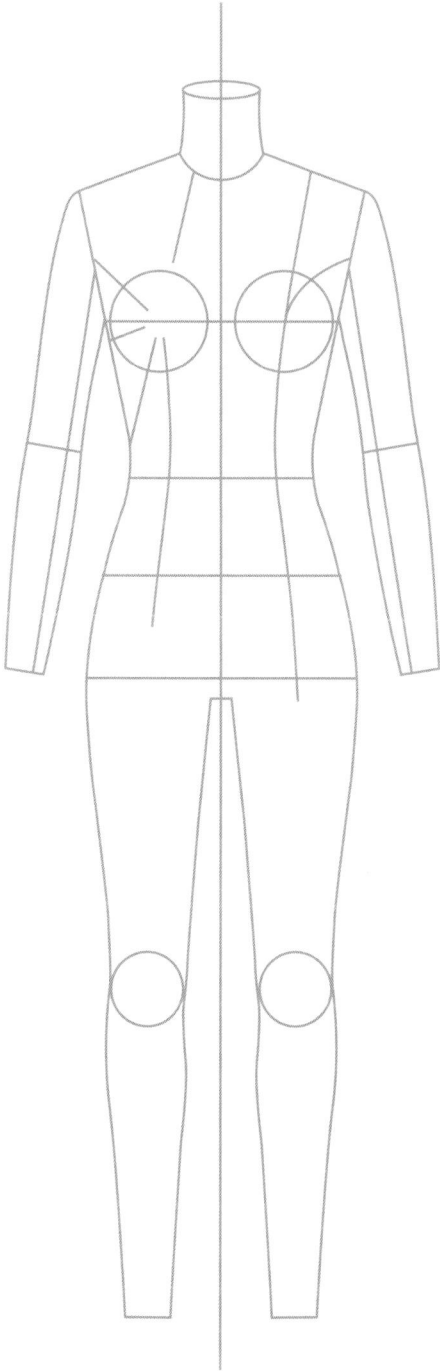

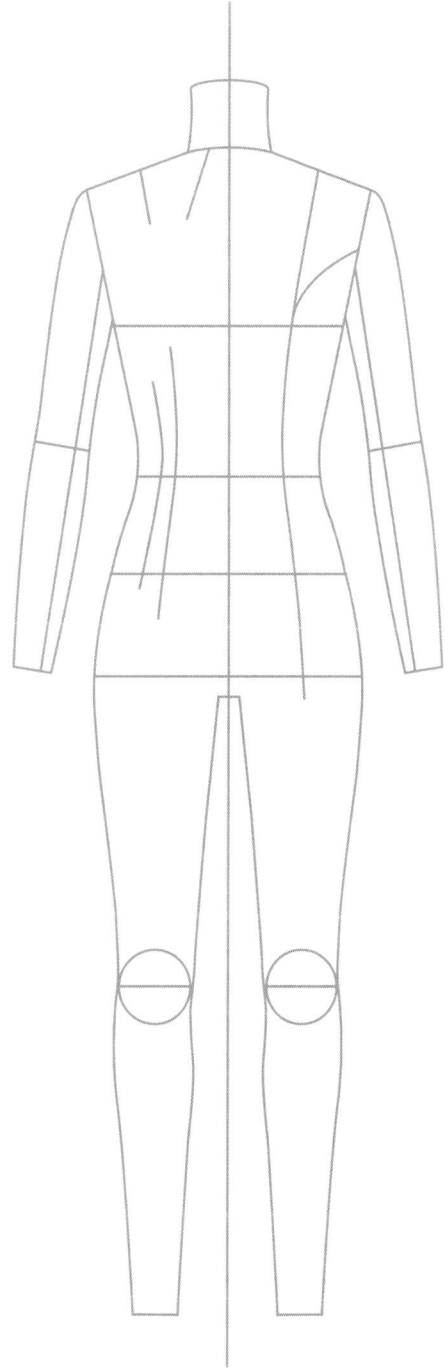

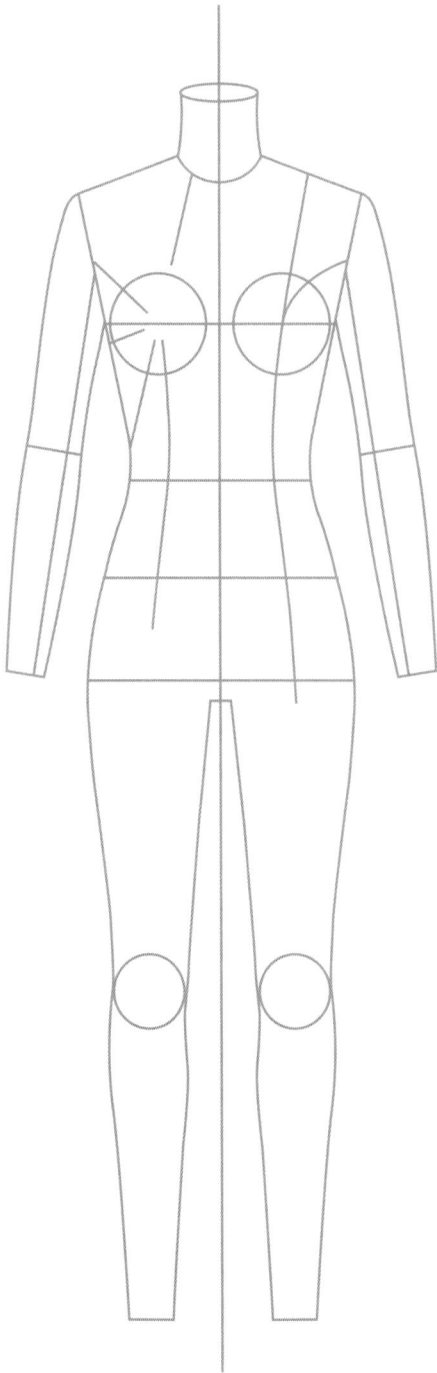

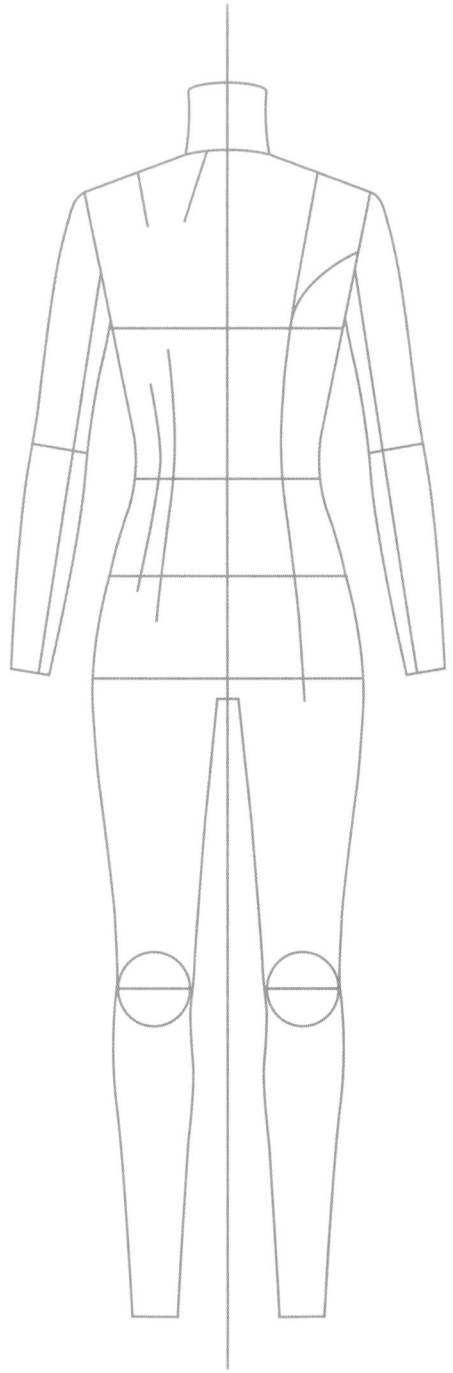

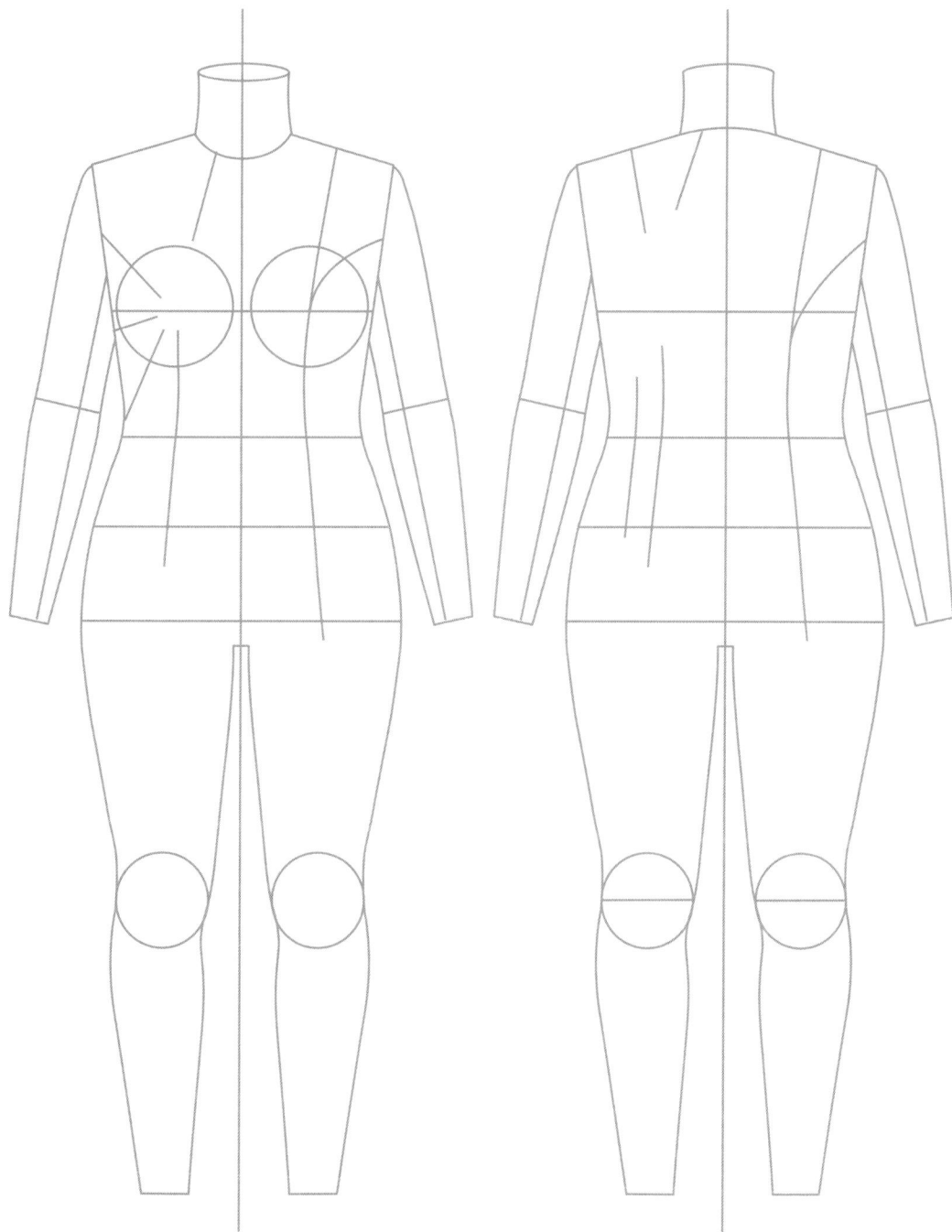

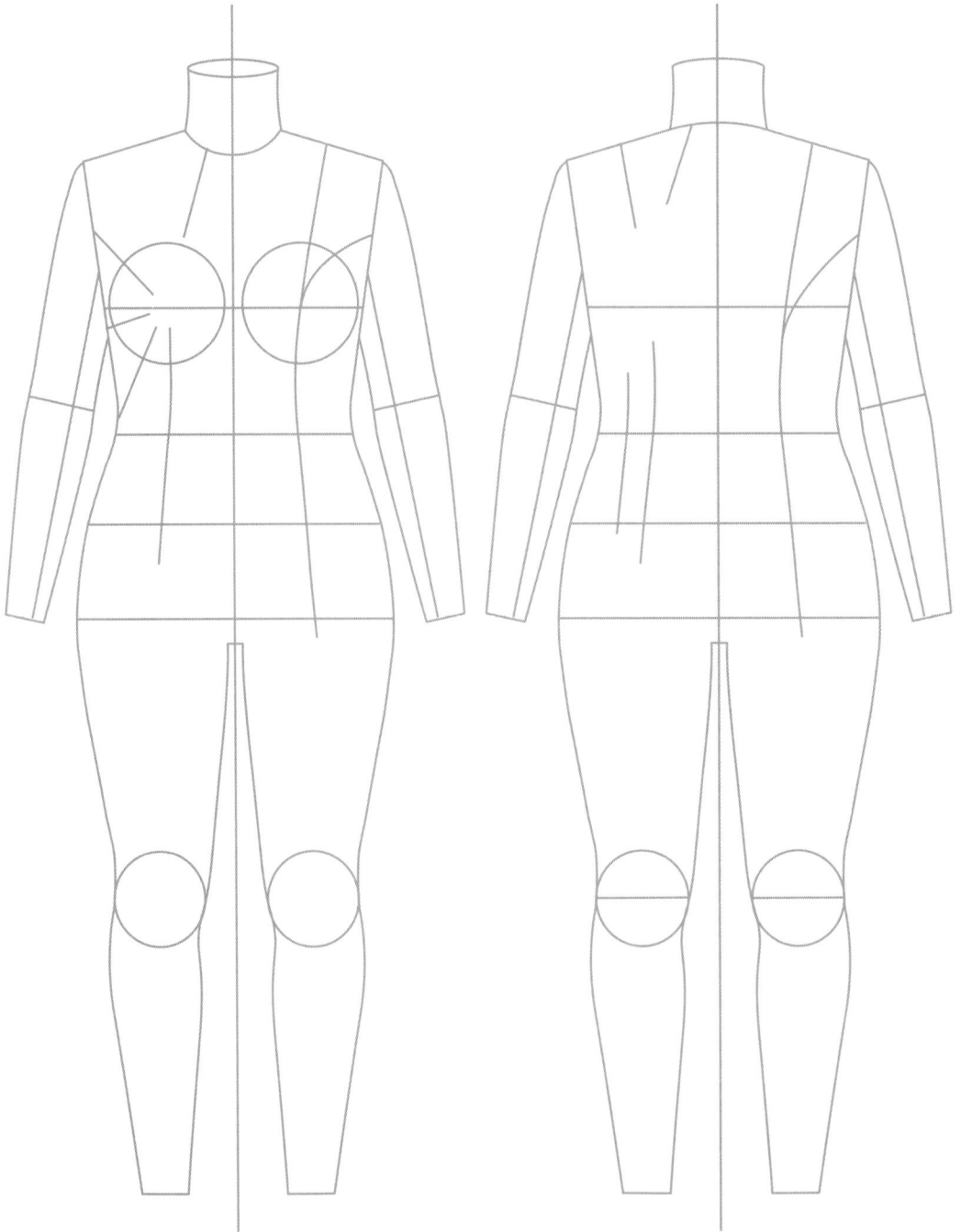

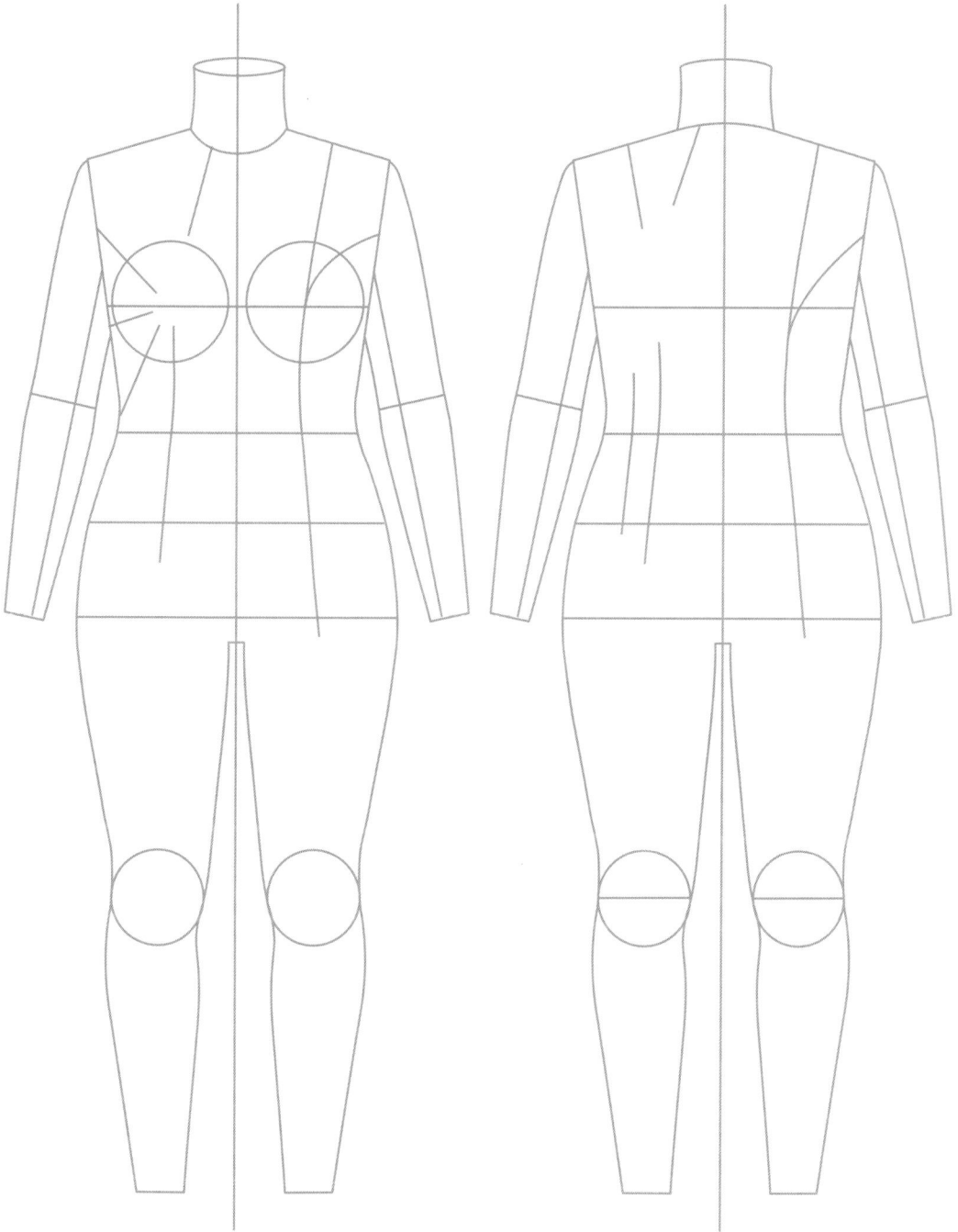

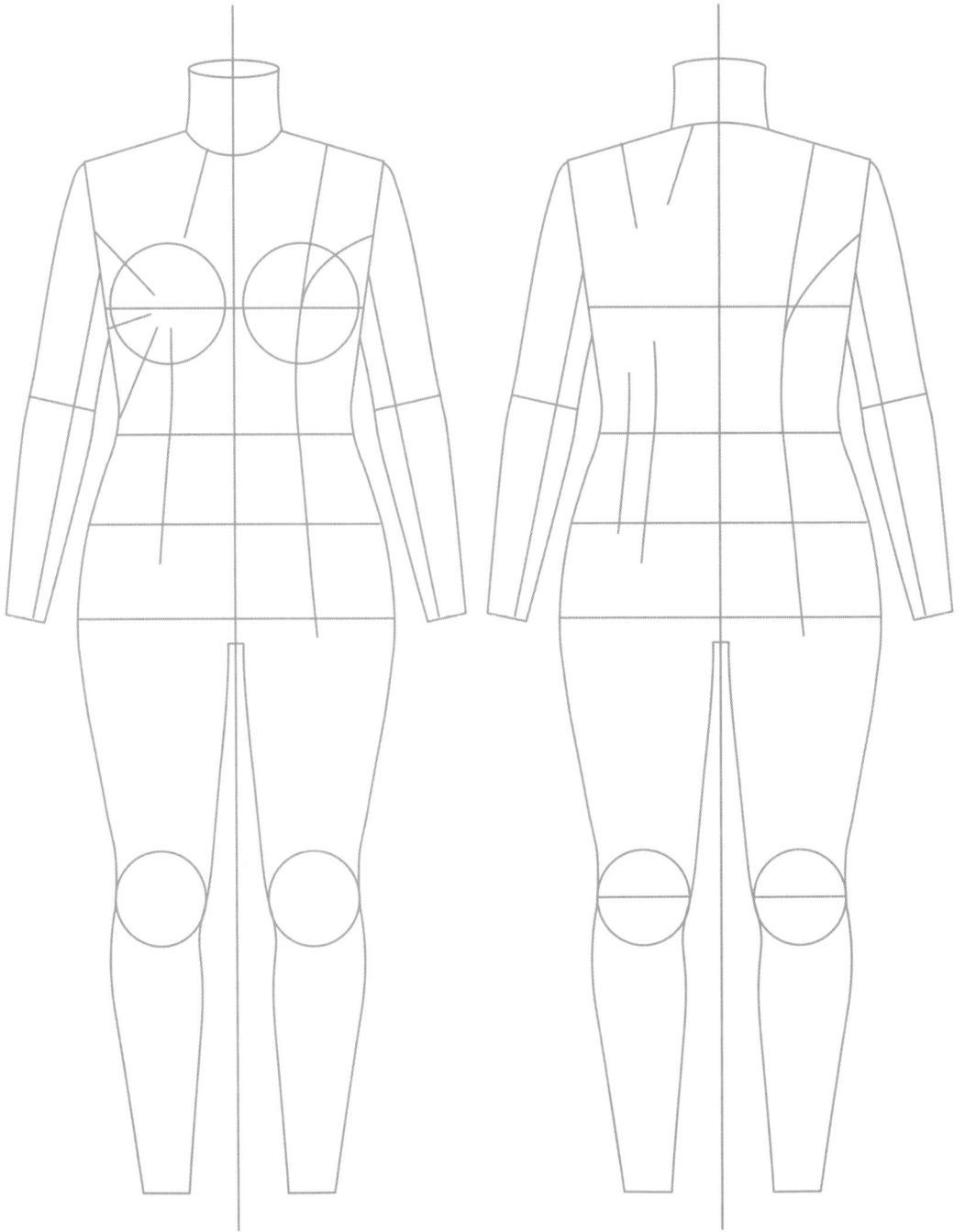

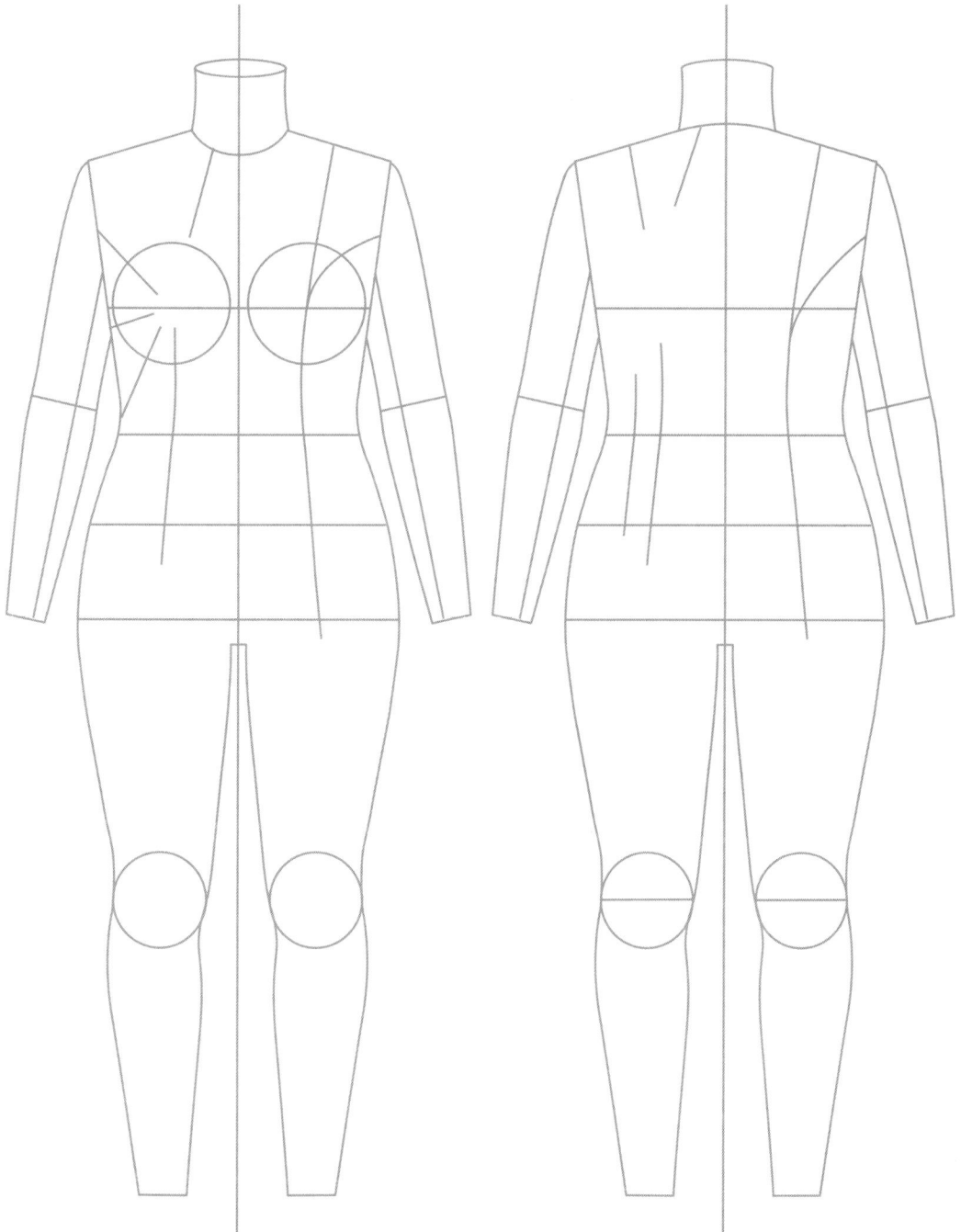

EXERCISES TO DESIGN ON THE FORM

- Drape a section, not a whole garment, in muslin on your dress form. Take a photo of the entire dress form. Print out the photo and draw right on top to expand upon the drape in different ways.

- Drape even smaller. Take a 12x12" (30x30 cm) piece of fabric and create drapes on top of a figure template. Take photos. Better yet, take a video, and then take screenshots of your favorite drapes.

- Pin twill tape to your dress form inspired by shapes found in your inspiration images. Drape partial or full garments using the twill tape as guides for style lines.

- Instead of a big blank piece of muslin, apply some fabric manipulations to the muslin before you use it. Fold the fabric up into rows and rows of pleats or tucks or ruffles or panels of smocking. Drape this piece on the form.

- Drape identical toiles in vastly different fabrics. This is also an excellent exercise to study fabrics. Try a light, stiff organza versus a heavy, slinky matte jersey. Try a thin, sharp cotton shirting versus a soft, spongy wool Melton or felt. Try draping with your final fabric or a similar, cheaper alternative.

- Another great fabric learning exercise is to drape identical designs on a form with one using the straight grain, and another on the bias.

- Cut a big geometric shape out of muslin. You can use a shape from your inspiration images. If you want to explore zero-waste cutting, make sure this piece is a big rectangle or triangle using the entire width of your fabric. Drape on a dress form with this shape. You can cut slices into the fabric but try not to cut *off* pieces of fabric. If you cut away pieces of fabric, try to incorporate them back into the design as pockets, patches, embellishments.

- Try taking something you don't wear anymore and take it to your dress form. Why don't you wear it anymore? Fix it.

- Take apart two dresses. You can pick them apart at the seams or cut them up however suits your fancy. Put the pieces back together on your dress form in a new way. Throw away as little as possible.

8

3-D DEVELOPMENT

This category covers doing anything to fabric to change its appearance or texture. Fabric manipulations can include, but are not limited to, darts, pleats, tucks, smocking, shell smocking, gathering/shirring/ruching, flounces, ruffles, padding, and quilting.

Fabric manipulations are different from embellishment, even though some people lump them all together. Embellishments are things applied on top of fabric to decorate the surface. These include embroidery, beading, sequins, paillettes, appliqué and patches, decorative topstitching, and adding trims like lace edging or fringe, piping, or cording.

Go through your sketchbook and make notes on what can be translated into fabric manipulations and/or embellishments. Pick up a book to learn how to embroider, seek out a class, or you can always sketch out your ideas and consult professionals.

The following pages detail exercises to help you design manipulations and embellishments.

EXERCISES TO DESIGN 3-D EFFECTS

1. Go buy some stuff and play! Go buy some yardage and fold it up, cut it up, sew it up. Go buy some beads and splay them out on a table and try arranging them in cool ways. Take photos and try again. Have your inspiration images in front of you so you're constantly referencing them, and those images are helping your brain.

2. Refer back to the exercises for designing prints in chapter 5 and apply them to fabric manipulations and embellishments. Refer also to the section on spin-off embellishments.

3. Cut up copies of your original inspiration and apply them to figure templates. Imagine the many ways those images can be translated in pleating and beading.

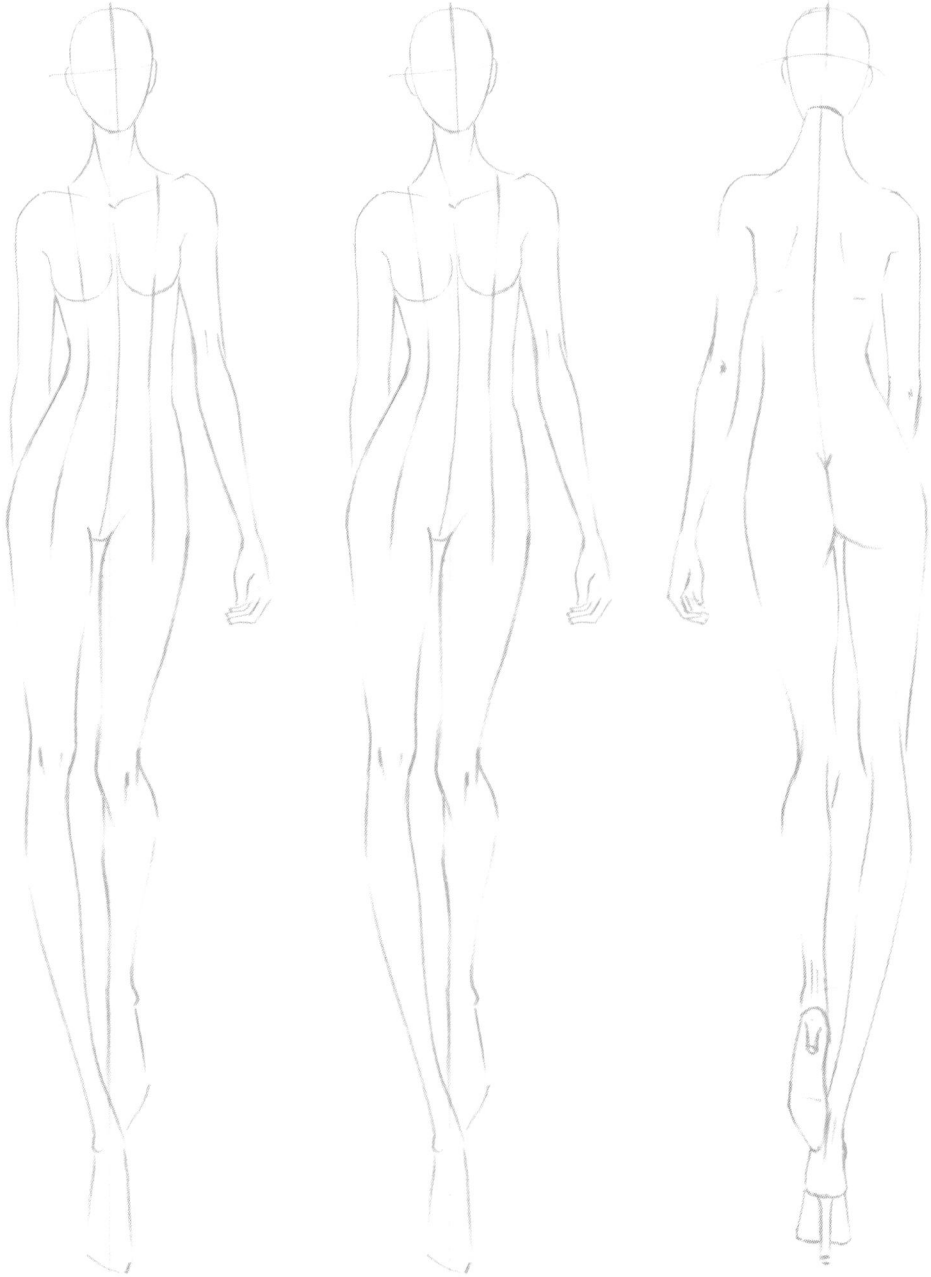

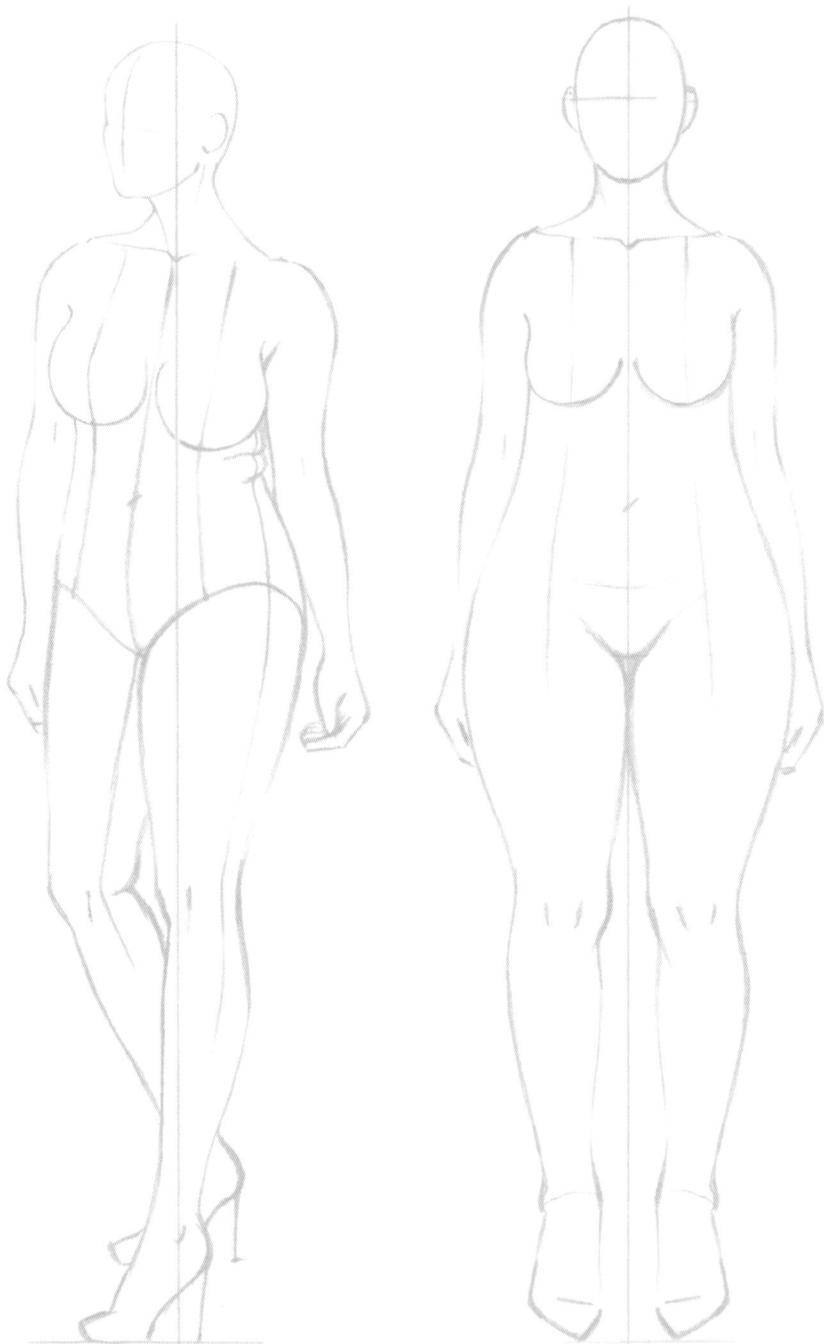

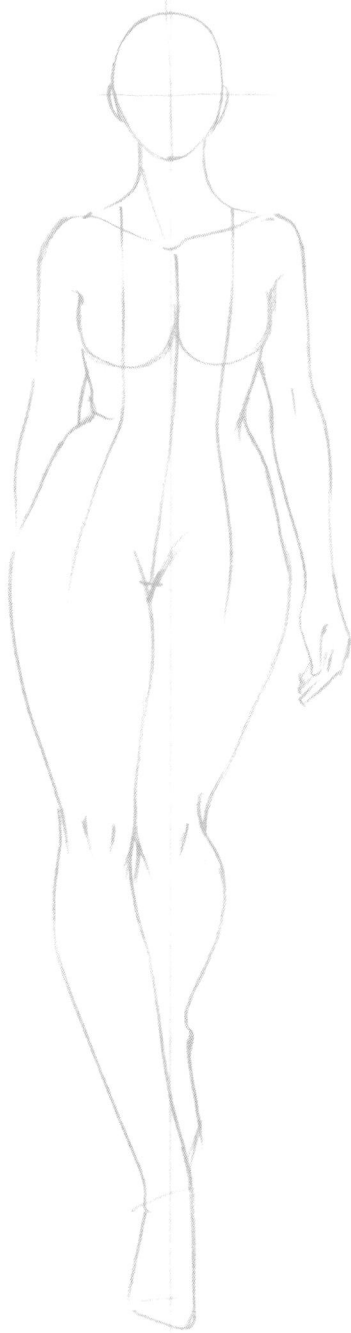

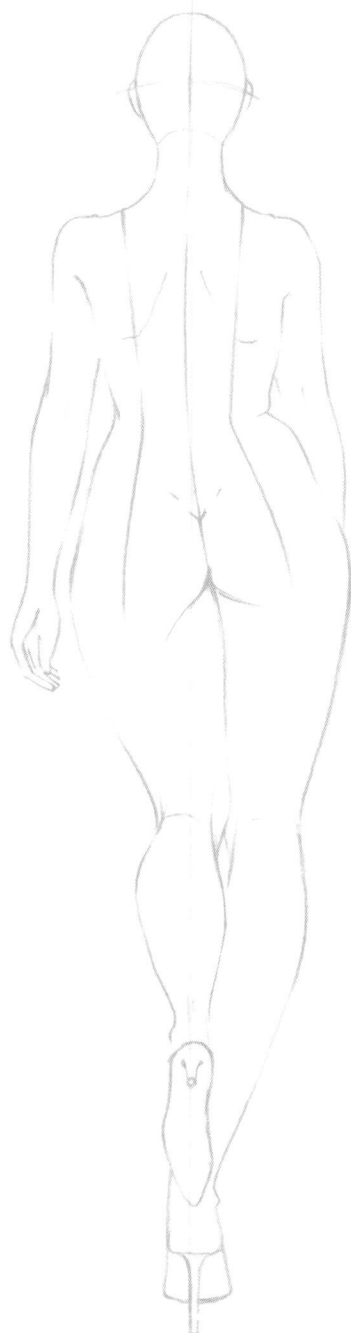

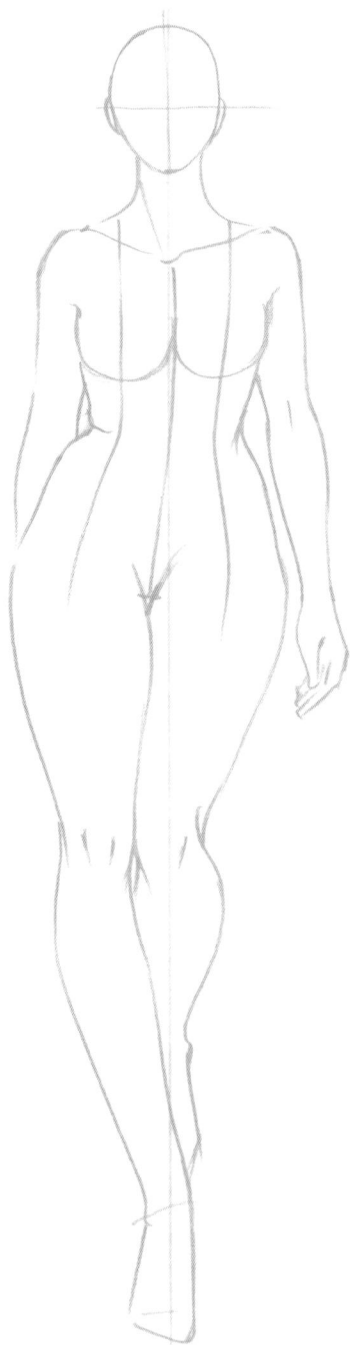

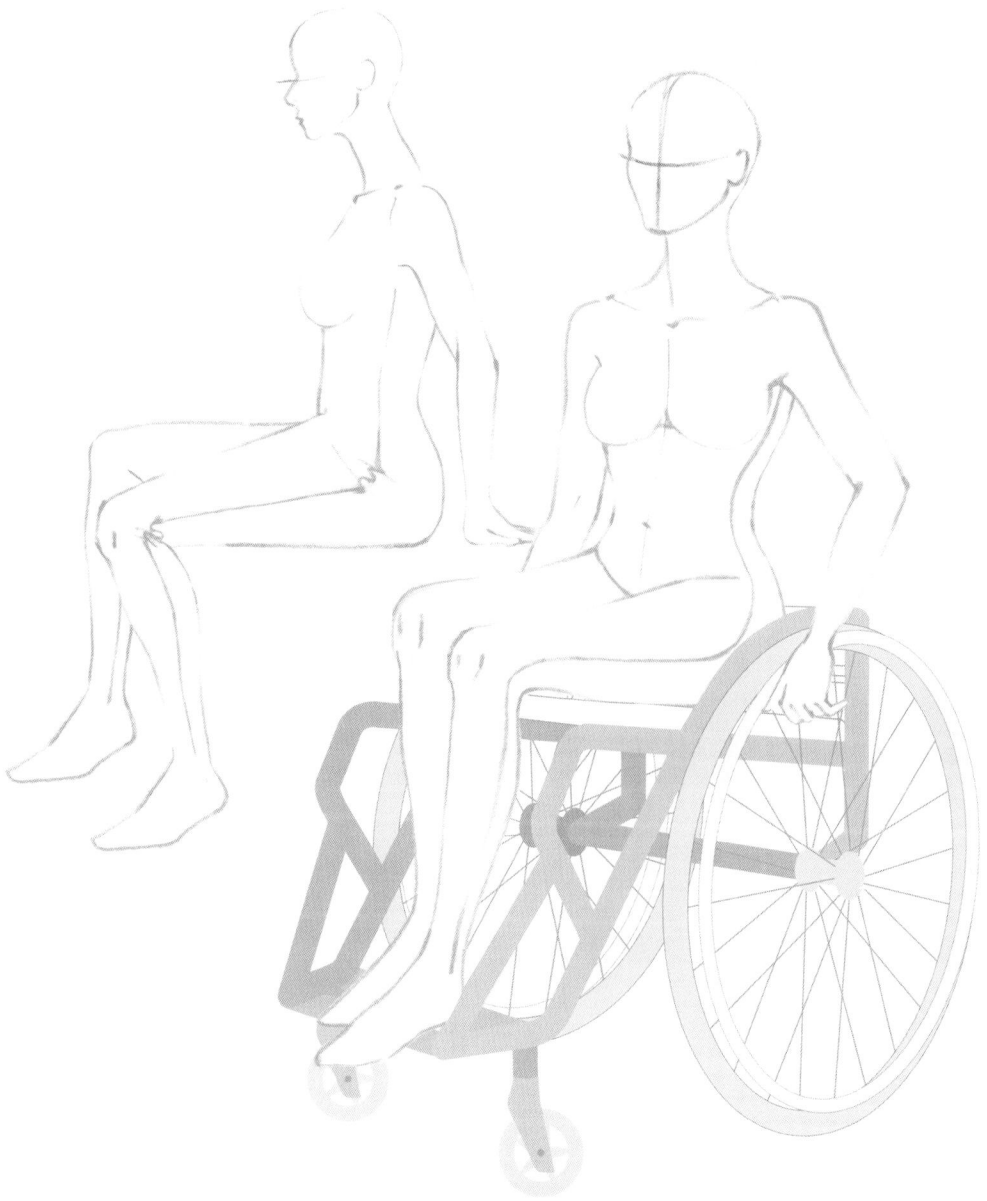

WORKING WITH SCRAP

Necessity is the mother of invention. Your brain can surprise you when pushed to its creative limits.

Go back to your notes and think about how you can be more sustainable in your materials and processes. Let's think about how you can use scrap in ways that look artful, not amateur.

One option is to use larger scraps of leather, suede, or nonwoven materials like felt to cut smaller pattern pieces. These materials have no grain, they are not woven or knit in a specific direction, so they can be cut up any which way. You can use these to cut pockets or more subtle details like a collar stand or under collar, or inside coat cuffs.

Explore options where you use the fabric in such a way that the grainline doesn't matter.

- I know of a company that used to buy large scrap from cutting factories and use that fabric to cut into strips and weave them into new fabrics. To be clear, they didn't do this themselves by hand, they hired a weaving company.

- I know of a different company that uses scrap to stitch cool fabric collages to the fronts of their shirts.

- Explore patchworking. You can sew pieces together to create a new fabric. *Jogakbo* is a Korean style of traditional patchwork that includes but also goes beyond a series of squares.

- You can use small pieces to make fabric flowers.

- You can also use small pieces to create appliqués.

- You can also use small pieces to make covered buttons.

- I've seen some cool effects with using scraps as stuffing in quilted fabrics, using sheer fabrics to show the colors inside. You can design around using scrap of a specific color story. The double effect is you use up scrap in a pretty easy way while also not using polyfill. I mean, you could shred scrap and use it as regular quilting stuffing, too, with regular opaque fabric. This effect would probably be better with a thicker fabric, to smooth out any lumps.

- You can make small accessories to either sell or include as a gift with purchase, such as scrunchies or bookmarks.

If you work with an aesthetic that fits, you can include a scrap with your purchase for mending. You know how beaded dresses often include a tiny baggie with spare beads and a bit of thread? You can sell your jeans with a square or two of denim for patching. You can post mending instructions on your website or social media, which is a handy way to get people to visit your site again. Maybe you can include patches of fun fabrics for mending kids' clothes.

LININGS

Linings serve both the aesthetics and function of the garment and should not be a sloppy afterthought. A good lining elevates the quality and perceived value of a garment. A good lining can elevate the design as well. Arguably the top function of linings is to cover the mess of raw edges and inner construction with something beautiful.

Linings add warmth. For winter coats, think about flannels and woolens. Sleeve linings should always be slippery so shirt sleeves of any fabric can slide into coat sleeves easily. You can line a coat with flannel in the body and something slippery in the sleeves. You can coordinate patterns and textures and solids to create a beautiful interior.

Linings add longevity to a garment by supporting the shell fabric and lending it strength. Lined garments crinkle less, as the extra thickness makes it harder to fold sharply. Lining protects the shell from your body's oils and sweat.

Match lining fiber content with your shell fiber content. Don't line a silk dress or wool jacket with a polyester lining! You will lose some of the benefits of silk or wool with a polyester lining, like silk and wool's breathability. Opt for a less expensive, thin silk like habotai.

You don't have to do a fiber-to-fiber match. You can just stick to categories, like using cellulose fabrics like cotton and linen for other cellulose fabric shells.

Alternatively, if you're trying to design something very lightweight, you must pay special attention to the shapes of facings and how seams are finished. Here are some swatch pages to help you catalog some lining fabrics.

fabric name:
fiber content:
description:

width:
vendor:
price & date:
colors:
notes:

fabric name:
fiber content:
description:

width:
vendor:
price & date:
colors:
notes:

fabric name:
fiber content:
description:

width:
vendor:
price & date:
colors:
notes:

fabric name: _____
fiber content: _____
description: _____
_____
width: _____
vendor: _____
price & date: _____
colors: _____
notes: _____
_____
_____
_____

fabric name: _____
fiber content: _____
description: _____
_____
width: _____
vendor: _____
price & date: _____
colors: _____
notes: _____
_____
_____
_____

fabric name: _____
fiber content: _____
description: _____
_____
width: _____
vendor: _____
price & date: _____
colors: _____
notes: _____
_____
_____

fabric name:

fiber content:

description:

width:

vendor:

price & date:

colors:

notes:

fabric name:

fiber content:

description:

width:

vendor:

price & date:

colors:

notes:

fabric name:

fiber content:

description:

width:

vendor:

price & date:

colors:

notes:

ALL THE TRIMMINGS

The word "trim" in fashion means pretty much anything on the garment that's not a type of fabric (self, lining, interfacing). Trim is the fringe on a shawl; trim is buttons, zippers, and snaps that close the jacket; trim is aglets on shoelaces: trim is piping and cording.

When designing a portfolio project, you don't have to design every lining, but showing one example lining on a coat or jacket would show your thoroughness as a designer. If you find an incredible fabric for a great contrast lining, you can include the swatch on your boards. Include trim on your boards that are pertinent to the design. A very special lace trim you've gathered into ruffles you use throughout the collection? Get that swatch. Little white buttons on a button-down shirt? Eh. We already know what those look like.

Use the following swatch pages to catalog cool trim for your collection.

fabric name: _____
fiber content: _____
description: _____
_____
width: _____
vendor: _____
price & date: _____
colors: _____
notes: _____
_____
_____

fabric name: _____
fiber content: _____
description: _____
_____
width: _____
vendor: _____
price & date: _____
colors: _____
notes: _____
_____
_____

fabric name: _____
fiber content: _____
description: _____
_____
width: _____
vendor: _____
price & date: _____
colors: _____
notes: _____
_____
_____

fabric name: _____
fiber content: _____
description: _____
_____
width: _____
vendor: _____
price & date: _____
colors: _____
notes: _____
_____
_____

fabric name: _____
fiber content: _____
description: _____
_____
width: _____
vendor: _____
price & date: _____
colors: _____
notes: _____
_____
_____

fabric name: _____
fiber content: _____
description: _____
_____
width: _____
vendor: _____
price & date: _____
colors: _____
notes: _____
_____
_____

fabric name: _____
fiber content: _____
description: _____
_____
width: _____
vendor: _____
price & date: _____
colors: _____
notes: _____
_____
_____
_____

fabric name: _____
fiber content: _____
description: _____
_____
width: _____
vendor: _____
price & date: _____
colors: _____
notes: _____
_____
_____
_____

fabric name: _____
fiber content: _____
description: _____
_____
width: _____
vendor: _____
price & date: _____
colors: _____
notes: _____
_____
_____
_____

MAKING SAMPLES

Start making samples of any design elements you want to test before you make a whole complete garment sample. It saves a lot of time and a lot of materials to test the artwork and small sections of the garment beforehand.

Some manipulations and embellishments should be sent out to professionals who specialize in these services. There are companies devoted to pleating, embroidery, debossing, and more. Create the artwork for the embroidery and get a sample done from a professional embroidery house. Your artwork should be drawn in a vector format. Send out yardage of your final fabric to get it professionally pleated so that the folds will hold permanently.

There are also companies that create patches and companies that apply appliqués to fabric. Patches are one single piece with all the design elements on that one piece. Appliqués are a design constructed by a series of fabric pieces sewn onto a background fabric.

If you're making a portfolio project, you should still make final art for your embroidery to include on your boards and test out some pleats in muslin. Samples you make will help recruiters visualize your designs better and you will show them you do know a thing or two about how a design gets made.

The following pages are deliberately left blank so you can work on final artwork, pin/staple some fabric manipulation samples, and make notes on process.

9

MERCHANDISING AND EDITING

Merchandising is part of designing and also part of editing. Looking at previous sales, fashion merchandisers analyze which silhouettes, fits, fabrications, and colorways have and have not sold well, and how this data should be incorporated in future collections.

You should absolutely repeat your best-selling whatever. Students and clients are often surprised by how much design houses repeat silhouettes, fabrics, and colors, even if they're not a category-specific brand like a denim house.

I cannot stress enough the difference between what goes down a runway and what gets sold in stores. This is not true of every brand, but the more editorial the brand's runway looks, the bigger the difference will tend to be. Look up your favorite designer and hunt down which pieces are sold in their own stores and other retailers.

Another aspect of merchandising is making sure you have a variety of styles for your customer. Not all your tops should be sleeveless. Not all your skirts should be maxis. Throw in a couple of different lengths. Edit out styles that are too similar to each other. The smaller a collection, the more you want to show a lot of ideas while keeping the collection cohesive.

Get organized. Divide your designs into categories and make sure you are designing an assortment within each category. I've developed some exercises to help you expand and merchandise your collection.

EXERCISE 1: MUSICAL CHAIRS

Design a garment and identify the design elements that make that dress special, such as contrast godets, a pattern of stitching, or sheer panels. Apply those elements to a jacket. And then pants. And then a top. You should recognize this sort of design rotation; it's very common.

EXERCISE 2: HOKEY POKEY

Design a garment and then remove an element. Adjust the design to balance it as necessary. Maybe you remove the collar and finish the neckline with some topstitching or binding. Take the new design and add a new element. That's three designs related to each other. Take the third design and remove a different element. Keep going.

This exercise works great when you want to deconstruct a classic, like a motorcycle jacket, shirt dress, or trench coat. You'll definitely want to start with a more complex design with a lot of elements.

EXERCISE 3: FUN FOR THE WHOLE FAMILY!

Design a garment and then adjust the garment for a younger customer, such as shortening the skirt. Adjust the original design for a grandma. Adjust the original design for the opposite gender. Adjust it again for a kid. Adjust it so it's more cutesy. Adjust it so it's more grown up and sophisticated. Adjust it for whoever your customer isn't.

What's the point of this? Understanding how to dress different customers will help you stay on track with your customer. This is for the next time you're at a fitting and think, "Why does this dress look matronly? How do I make this look more youthful?"

EXERCISE 4: FASHION PLATES

Select four previously designed garments. Choose the same category (all dresses, all jackets, etc.). Cut them apart and make four new garments with the pieces. The aim is to have some part of each of the four previous garments in each new garment. The point is to push you to use the same design elements and motifs in a new way. Do you remember the '80s toy Fashion Plates? Like that.

EXERCISE 5: ANALYZE A DESIGNER

Pick a designer or brand, and pick several seasons of collections (a variety of seasons—spring, fall, resort, pre-fall) over several years. Scroll through and study them. Start jotting down design elements you see and make three lists:

1. Elements you see throughout only one collection

2. Elements you see in many collections

3. Elements you see very rarely or only once

These elements can be a specific silhouette or shape, a certain hem, a color story, a motif (like bows)—so many things. Just look for repeats.

Run this analysis on a few different designers you admire so you can learn about how brands merchandise their collections (and what their house codes are).

Elements in one collection	Elements in many collections	Elements you see very rarely

EXERCISE 6: EDIT SOMEONE ELSE'S COLLECTION

Sometimes we feel a little precious about our work and find it difficult to "trash" things. I know because I've been there. Select a collection and download the photos. Open them up in Photoshop. Take out all the outfits that don't work. Try pairing tops with different bottoms to make new outfits. Practice editing out half the looks to make a more cohesive collection of the best pieces that still show variety.

EXERCISE 7: EDIT AN OLDER COLLECTION OF YOUR OWN

Pull out all the sketches from an older collection of your own, including the designs that you edited out before. Again, you may feel less precious about an older collection. Re-edit and re-merchandise your collection. Fresh, better-developed eyes can create a better collection off old designs with some minor alterations.

EXERCISE 8: ORGANIZING FOR PRESENTATION

Whether that presentation is portfolio boards, a runway show, or a series of lookbook photos, you want to present your collection in the best light possible.

Gather up all the sketches from your project. Make a set of copies. Cut all the copies in half and tape them together again creating new combinations of tops and bottoms. Pair different jackets and coats with different outfits. Layer in new ways.

If your collection is well merchandised, each of your tops should coordinate well with several different bottoms and vice versa. Each jacket or coat should work with several outfits.

You may think this is about styling outfits, but this comes before that. If you have a random blouse that doesn't work with anything else in your collection, don't even bother making a sample. If it's still amazing, make like a Zoë-esque trash panda and pocket it for another day.

Again, pay attention to creating a cohesive collection that still offers visual variety. And while the point isn't styling, this exercise will help with styling for your presentation without making your model try on 3,921 outfit variations.

EXERCISE 9: EXPLORING COLORWAYS

The last consideration is which color to present each garment. Every garment, except for the occasional editorial piece, should be offered in multiple colorways. Gather up all your sketches and make a set of miniature copies. Color your garments quickly. Neatness does not count here. Check to see which colors from your color story look good on which garment. This step is especially important for garments with any color blocking. Set up your outfits in a lineup for a practice presentation.

10
BEYOND DESIGN
PROCESS FOR BRANDS

You can photocopy these flats templates and draw directly on top by hand; or you can scan them into Adobe Illustrator, lock them in a template layer, and draw your flats on top. Adobe Illustrator flats are always preferable but if you work for yourself, at least make sure to use a ruler and make your flats clean and symmetrical.

Final flats for tech packs are the finishing stage of design leading into product development. This is when you iron out the little, but still important, details like button size and spacing, type of zipper, exact size of pleats, and how many pockets you can fit on and in a coat.

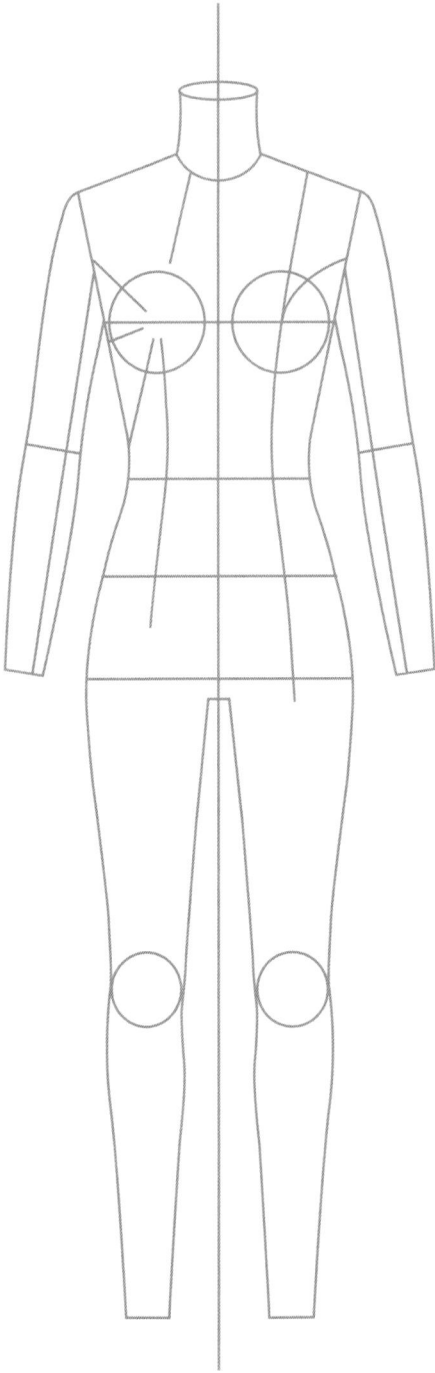

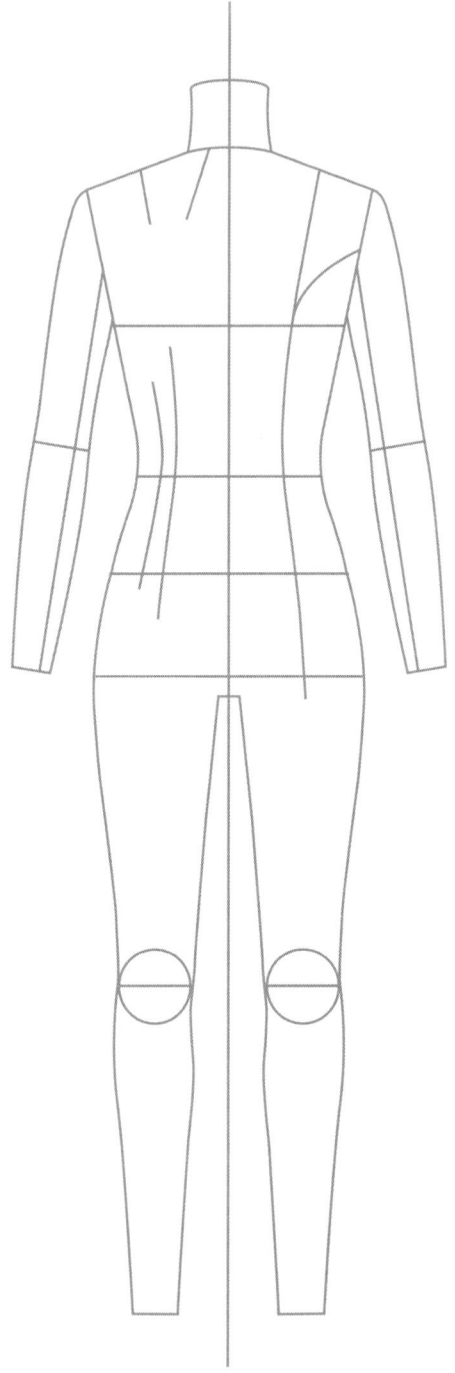

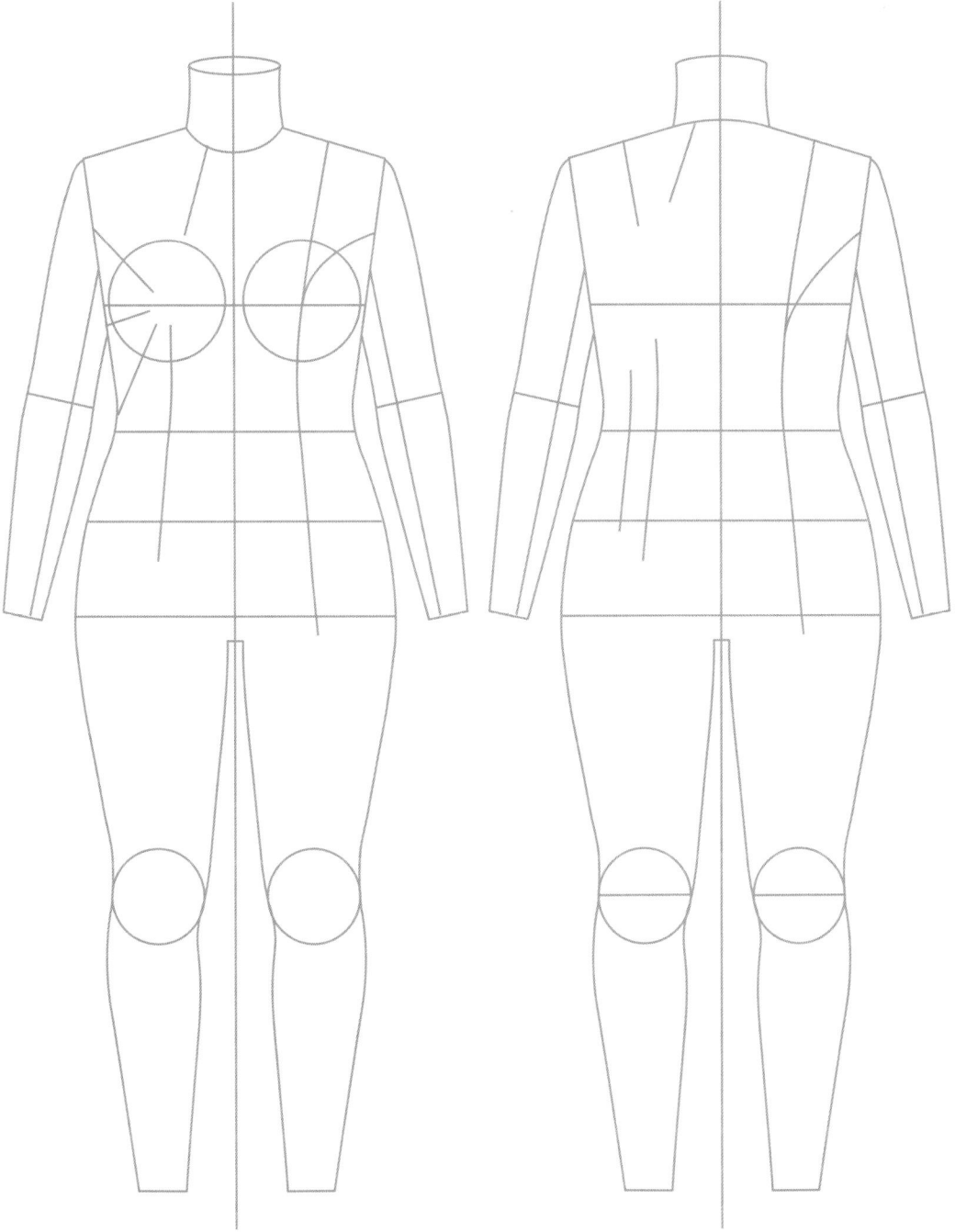

11
PORTFOLIOS

This chapter is for people who want to make a beautiful portfolio in hopes of getting a job at a bigger company. A few things to consider when planning your portfolio:

- You'll want three to five projects for your portfolio. No one's going to look at all five. You want a variety of projects that you can show at different interviews depending on the kind of job. Your portfolio will likely become more focused as you progress in your career and you find your specialties.

- Not every project needs to be extremely elaborate. You can add all or one of the optional boards I list below.

- Not every project needs to feature complete outfits. There are many, many companies that design only one category of clothes, like outerwear or swimsuits.

- Think about what kinds of jobs you want to apply for and what skills you want to emphasize.

- Show you can design for different seasons, different price points, and different bodies.

At minimum, for each project, you will need a mood board, color and fabric board, a board with the illustrations of your outfits, and a board with front and back flats of each design. Optionally, you can add photos of finished garments, a board with 3-D samples, a little bound book of sketches you edited out (a.k.a. a croquis book), and individual pages detailing each outfit (figure illustration, flats, swatches, details).

Use the following blank pages to plan out your portfolio boards.

The following pages feature garment sketches to practice your renderings in preparation for your portfolio illustrations. Full rendering tutorials can be found in *Fashion School in a Book: Design & Illustration for the Beginner and the Brand.*

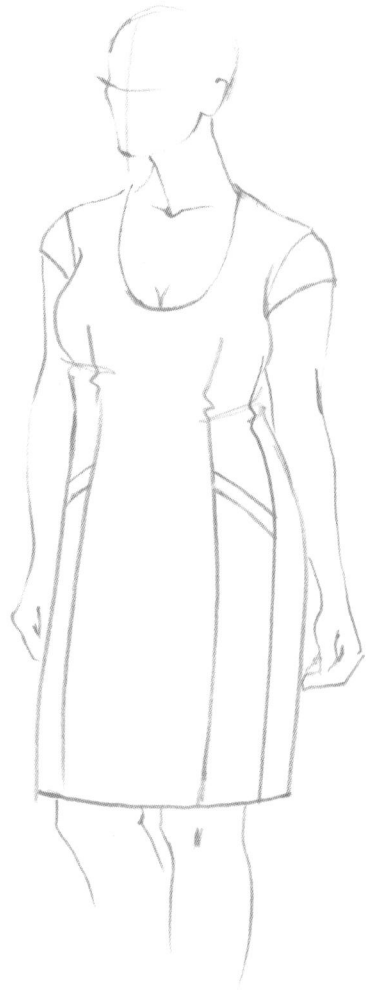

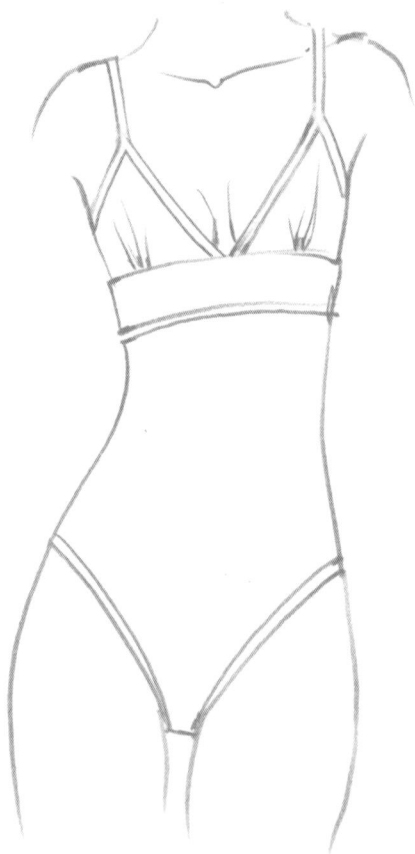

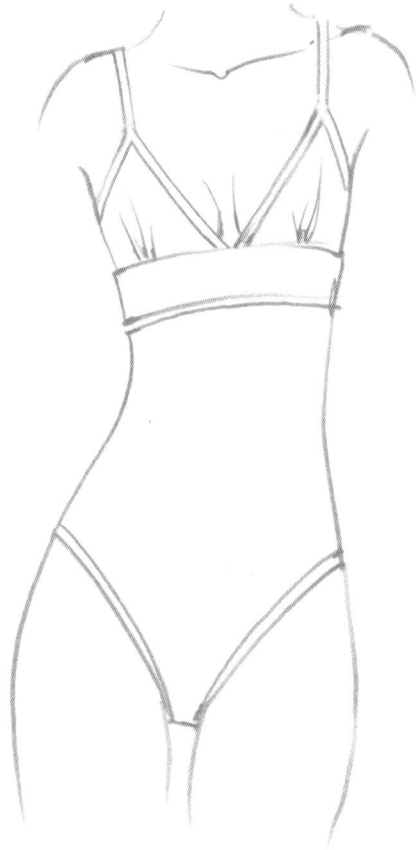

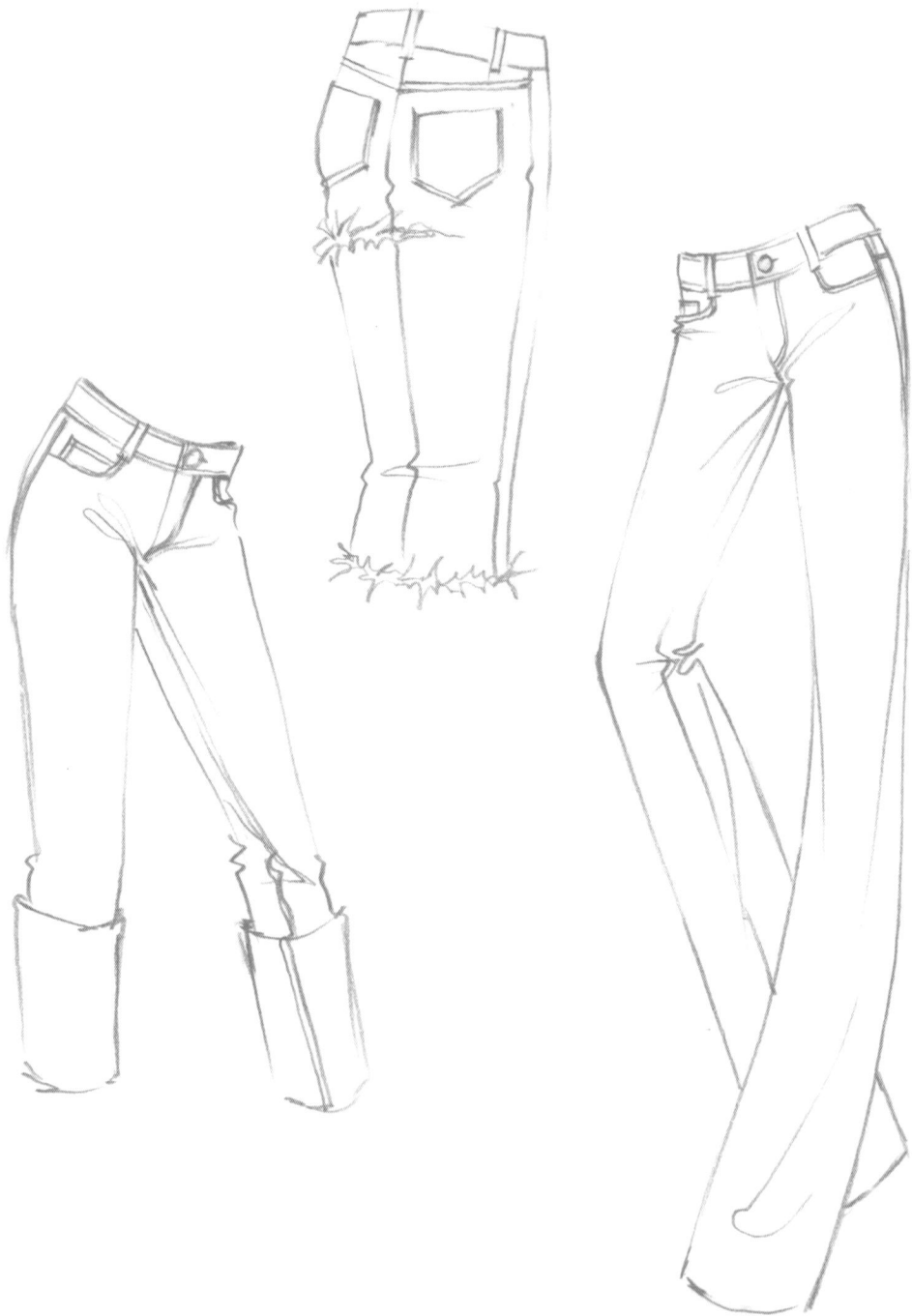

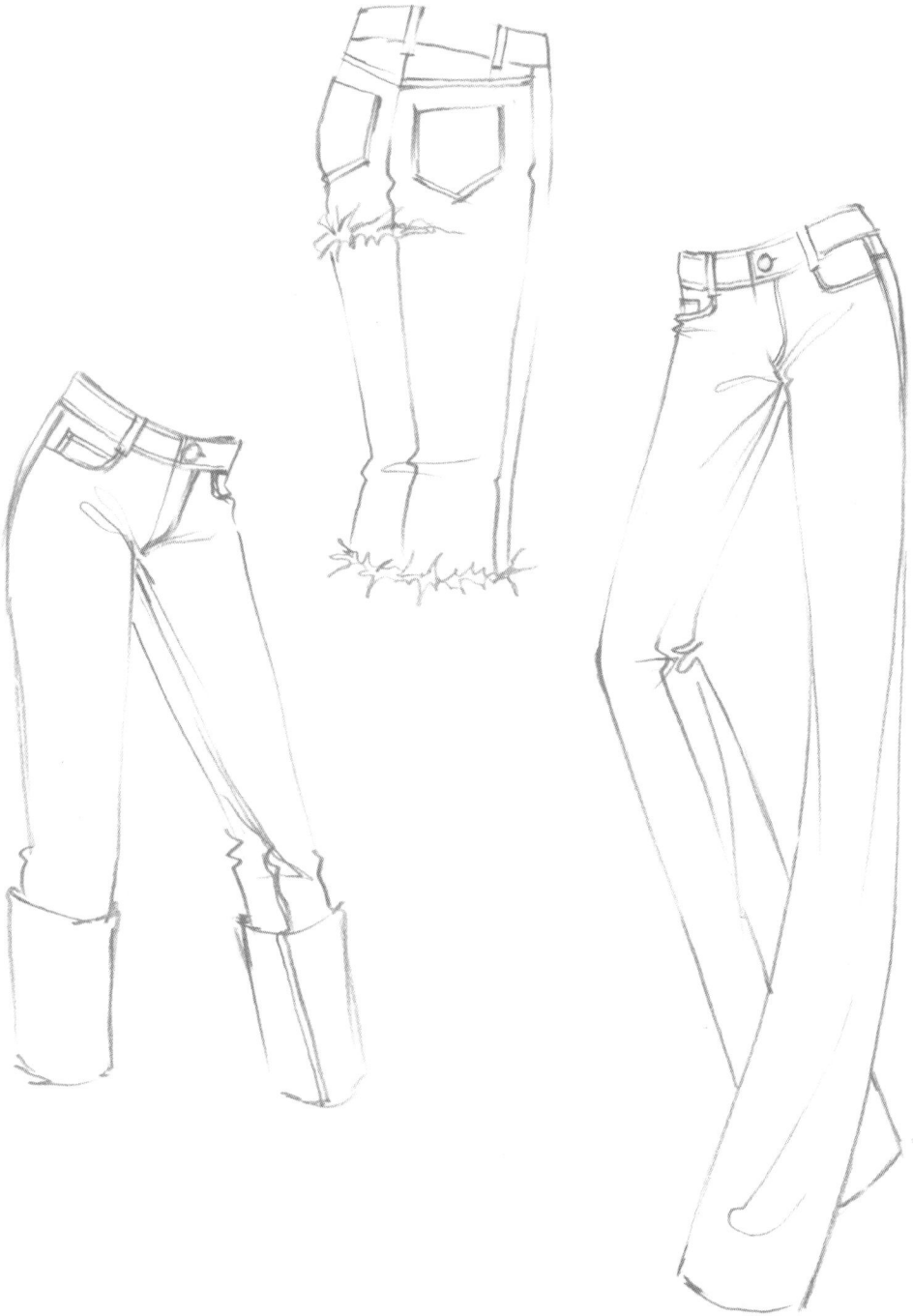

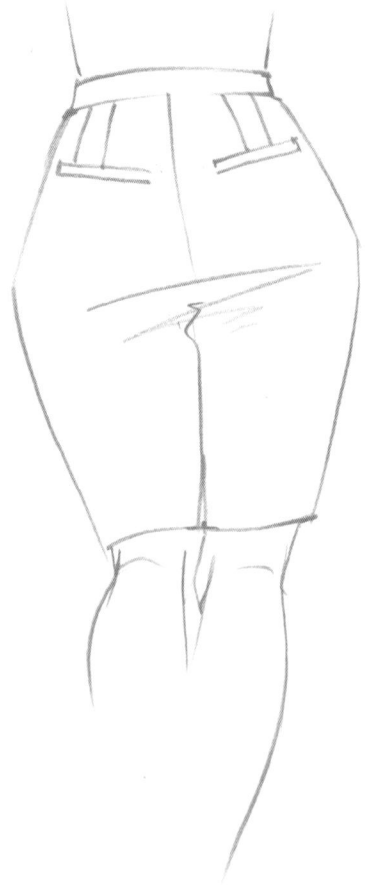

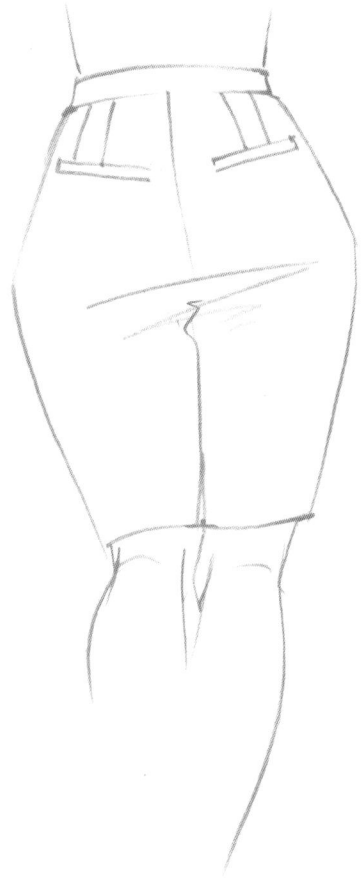

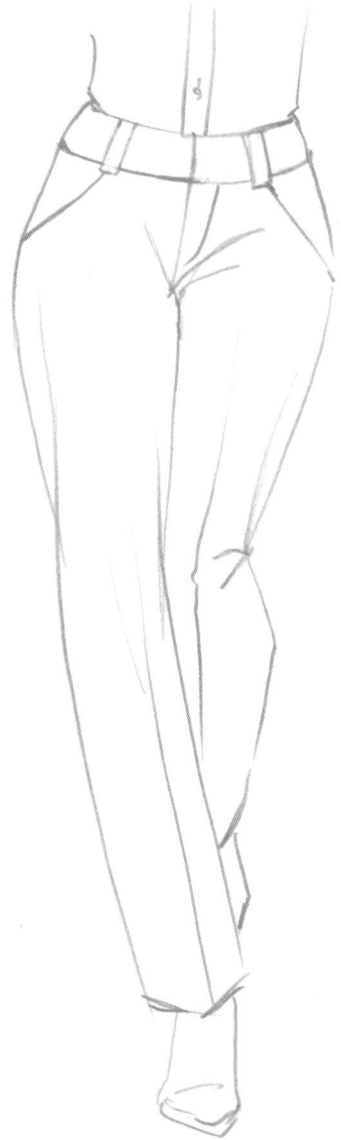

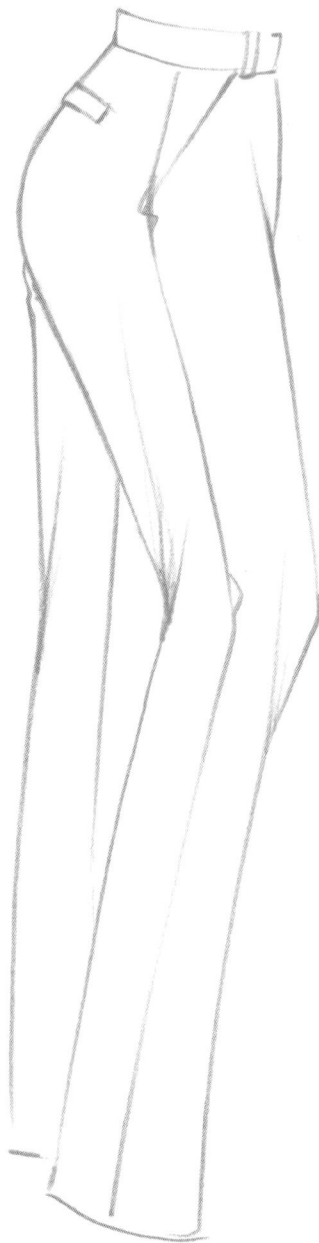

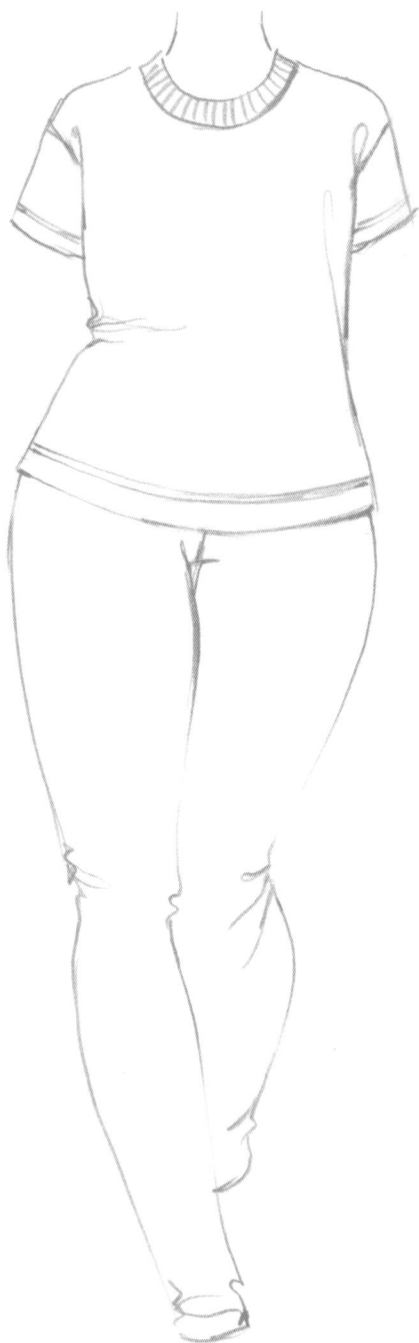

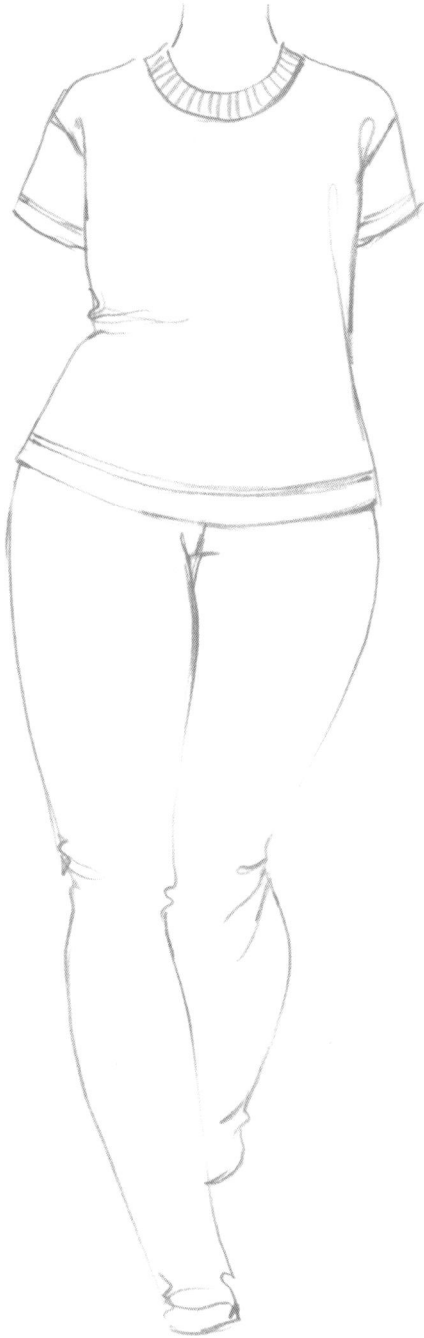